Quality
Teaching
Through
Professional
Development

Series Editors:
John T. Greer
Donn W. Gresso

Principals Taking
ACTION
Series

Joint publications of
THE NATIONAL ASSOCIATION OF SECONDARY SCHOOL PRINCIPALS
and
CORWIN PRESS, INC.

Rethinking Student Discipline
Alternatives That Work
　　Paula M. Short, Rick Jay Short and Charlie Blanton

Thriving on Stress for Success
　　Walter H. Gmelch and Wilbert Chan

Creating Safe Schools
What Principals Can Do
　　Marie Somers Hill and Frank W. Hill

Quality Teaching Through Professional Development
　　Allan A. Glatthorn and Linda E. Fox

Allan A. Glatthorn
Linda E. Fox

Quality
Teaching
Through
Professional
Development

CORWIN PRESS, INC.
A Sage Publications Company
Thousand Oaks, California

For information address:

Corwin Press, Inc.
A Sage Publications Company
2455 Teller Road
Thousand Oaks, California 91320
E-mail: order@corwin.sagepub.com

SAGE Publications Ltd.
6 Bonhill Street
London EC2A 4PU
United Kingdom

SAGE Publications India Pvt. Ltd.
M-32 Market
Greater Kailash I
New Delhi 110 048 India

Printed in the United States of America

Library of Congress Cataloging-in-Publication Data

Glatthorn, Allan A., 1924-
    Quality teaching through professional development / Allan A.
Glatthorn, Linda E. Fox.
        p. cm.—(Principals taking action series)
    Includes bibliographical references and index.
    ISBN 0-8039-6273-8 (alk. paper).—ISBN 0-8039-6274-6 (pbk.:
alk. paper)
        1. Teachers—In-service training. 2. Teachers. 3. Teaching.
I. Fox, Linda E. II. Title. III. Series.
LB1731.G556 1995
371.1'46—dc20   95-21332

This book is printed on acid-free paper.

96 97 98 99   10 9 8 7 6 5 4 3 2 1

Corwin Press Production Editor: Tricia K. Bennett

Contents

List of Boxes, Figures, and Tables

Boxes

Figures

Tables

Preface

This book is written primarily for principals and the teachers they serve. Both groups are very much dissatisfied with conventional supervision. Principals are dissatisfied because it does not get the results intended: Teachers teach as they have always taught. Teachers are unhappy with it because they see it as a meaningless and intrusive ritual.

The problem, of course, is not with the basic strategies employed: Observing and conferring are useful tools. The real problem is that all teachers, regardless of experience and competence, receive the same superficial treatment—two observations a year, followed by debriefing conferences of "good news" and "bad news."

The solution offered in this book has several features. First, it is individualized: Teachers get the support and services they need based upon their experience, their competence, and their level of motivation. Second, it is multifaceted: The services available to teachers go beyond the limited "observe-confer" cycle of clinical supervision. Also, it is practical, addressing the realities that principals and teachers face in the complex world of schools. Finally, it is scholarly, drawing on the best current research on teaching, teacher development, and team leadership.

The book opens by laying the foundations for teacher development. The first chapter explains what is known about teaching and uses that knowledge to identify four general groups of teachers: productive teachers, who are highly motivated and skilled; novice teachers, who are still mastering the basic skills of teaching; marginal teachers, experienced teachers who still demonstrate serious deficiencies; and passive teachers, who are competent but unmotivated.

The second chapter explains the kind of work environment that all teachers and principals should have, an environment that we term a *learning community.* In such a learning community, growth and development flourish in a collaborative culture. Chapter 3 explains how to organize that learning community for individualizing developmental services. However, rather than prescribing one set of structures for all schools, the chapter explains the basic principles needed and presents a process that can be used in developing homegrown structures.

Chapters 4, 5, 6, and 7 explain how principals can foster the development of the four groups of teachers identified. Each of these chapters begins by explaining the characteristics and needs of the group considered. The chapter then explains what services are needed and how they can best be provided.

Chapter 8 focuses on the nonteaching professional staff, the nurses, librarians, counselors, social workers, and classified staff ignored in all the standard texts on supervision. They can make a valuable contribution to any school if their developmental needs are addressed. The book ends by explaining how principals can develop the resources needed to accomplish the goals identified.

Acknowledgments

The book owes much to several individuals. We would like first of all to acknowledge our gratitude to all those teachers whom we have served and the principals with whom we have worked; most of what we have learned about teacher development has come from them.

We owe a special debt to the teachers and administrators who reviewed initial drafts of these chapters: Lynn Bradshaw, Assistant

Superintendent, Wilson (North Carolina) County Schools; Steven Scroggs, Principal, Teachers Memorial School, Lenoir (North Carolina) County Schools; Dale Glatthorn, Harrison Elementary School, Philadelphia; Julie Fairley, Director of Secondary Education, Douglas County (Colorado) Public Schools; Tony Harrison, Principal, Washington (North Carolina) High School.

Finally, we acknowledge the productive guidance we received from Donn Gresso and John Greer, editors of this series. They first suggested the need for this work and helped us improve its quality.

Allan A. Glatthorn
East Carolina University

Linda E. Fox
Elizabeth High School

About the Authors

Allan A. Glatthorn is Professor in the School of Education, East Carolina University, where he teaches graduate courses in curriculum, supervision, and school administration. For more than 20 years he was a high school teacher, department chair, and principal. He has written 15 professional books in his areas of expertise: His most recent book is *Developing a Quality Curriculum.* He has consulted with more than 200 school systems in planning and implementing programs in teacher development.

Linda E. Fox is currently the Principal of Elizabeth High School in Elizabeth, Colorado. She taught for 15 years in Illinois and Colorado, in grades 7 through 12, and has served as a school administrator for 11 years. In 1992, she served on the Colorado Achievement Commission Task Force on Management and Organization and has been chair of the Curriculum Committee of the National Association of Secondary School Principals. She is a doctoral student at the University of Colorado at Denver.

Dedication

We dedicate this work to some very special people. Both of us feel deeply indebted to all the administrators and teachers from whom we have learned. Linda Fox dedicates the book to Phil, with gratitude for his steadfast support, and to Brian, Jeff, and Mavis, for their inspiration. Allan Glatthorn dedicates the work to all his brothers and sisters— and especially to his wife Barbara: They have all been an unfailing source of support.

Building the Knowledge Base
for Quality Teaching

Fostering quality teaching can best be accomplished if supervisory strategies and approaches are built on a sound knowledge base. This first chapter provides such a base by reviewing what is currently known about quality teaching and teachers' growth and development and then discussing the implication of these analyses for the principal's approach to teacher supervision. Understanding the nature of quality teaching clarifies the goals that are the focus of all supervisory services. And knowing how teachers develop provides insight into what approaches are most effective.

The Nature of Quality Teaching

Quality teaching is defined as teaching that maximizes learning for all students. *Learning*, in this definition, is comprehensive growth—

TABLE 1.1 The Levels of Teaching Skill

| Behavior | Level of Skill | | |
Categories	Basic	Intermediate	Advanced
Model of teaching	Uses direct instruction	Uses model recommended by experts in field	Uses several models, especially constructivism
Curriculum	Implements district guide	Integrates within subject	Integrates two or more subjects, providing for enrichment and remediation
Content knowledge	Avoids content errors	Demonstrates sound and current content knowledge	Enables students to understand deep structure of subject
Classroom climate	Maintains orderly environment, uses most of class time for learning	Maintains learning-focused environment, maximizes time on task	Varies environment to suit learning goal, providing for cooperative interaction, relates time use to learning priorities

continuing development in knowledge, skills, and attitudes. Comprehensive growth is accomplished by teachers who have mastered the basic skills of teaching and are moving forward in their development of intermediate and advanced skills.

Levels of Teaching Skill

This book presents a conceptualization of teaching skills as embracing three levels: basic, intermediate, and advanced. (The development of this conceptual framework was stimulated by a review of one developed by Leithwood, 1992.)

TABLE 1.1 (Continued)

Behavior Categories	Level of Skill		
	Basic	*Intermediate*	*Advanced*
Lesson structure	Provides overview, states objectives	Also makes transitions effectively and summarizes lesson	Varies lesson structure when necessary to encourage discovery
Learning activities	Provides activities that relate to objectives	Varies activities	Emphasizes active learning assessment
Assessment	Checks for understanding	Also uses assessment data to modify instruction	Uses authentic assessment measures, giving feedback to students
Communication	Explains clearly, questions effectively	Also uses student answers to advance discussion	Also structures discussion to foster student-student interaction

As Table 1.1 indicates, teaching skills are conceptualized as including eight categories of behavior. The first is the model of teaching that the teacher uses most of the time, either as a result of decision making or training. The second is how the teacher uses the district curriculum guide in planning and teaching. Next is the teacher's mastery of content knowledge. The fourth category involves the classroom climate and environment for learning. Fifth is the type and extent of lesson structure, the way the teacher organizes instruction. The sixth category embraces the teaching-learning activities provided. How the teacher assesses learning is the next category. The final category involves the communication processes, focusing on the teacher's use of explaining, questioning, and responding.

In each of these categories, it is hypothesized that teachers move through three levels, each one more complex and more comprehensive than the preceding one. Most novice teachers (as well as many less competent experienced teachers) are at the basic level. Teachers who have mastered the basic skills move on to the intermediate level if they are motivated, perhaps about from the 3rd to the 6th year of teaching. Many seem to get stuck at that intermediate level. Expert teachers are functioning at the advanced level. Obviously, an individual teacher's progress will probably be uneven; a teacher may be functioning at the basic level with respect to student assessment and at the intermediate level in lesson structure.

Although the model itself has not been validated by research studies, it draws from a considerable body of literature (see Glatthorn, 1993). As noted in succeeding chapters, the model should be useful to principals and teachers as they reflect about improvement goals.

Models of Teaching

Special mention should be made of the first category, models of teaching, in that most models subsume many of the other seven categories identified in Table 1.1. In general, the research indicates that beginning teachers rely on the direct instruction model, usually formulated as Hunter's (1984) "six-step lesson plan," which included the following components: anticipatory set, presentation, checking for understanding, guided practice, independent practice, and closure. Although she denied that her work was an attempt to prescribe how teachers should teach every lesson, many school systems used the Hunter model as a basis for teacher evaluation and staff development, thereby reinforcing a "cookbook" approach to teaching.

The teacher at the intermediate level has moved away from reliance on direct instruction and more often uses a model recommended by experts in a particular subject field. Thus, many teachers of science use what Joyce and Weil (1986) term a *scientific inquiry model*. Most elementary teachers have embraced a *whole language* approach to teaching language arts. Teachers at the advanced level vary the model of teaching, depending on the learners and the learning goals. Most teachers at the advanced level are probably using what has come to be termed as a *constructivist* model of teaching. This particular model is so important that it requires special examination here.

The Constructivist Model. Rather than being one more educational fad, constructivism seems to be a major rethinking of learning and teaching, one that will have a lasting impact on both curriculum and instruction. The following discussion explains the essential principles of constructivism; principals wishing to learn more about this model should consult the references noted. (The discussion that follows draws chiefly from Berryman, 1991; Brooks & Brooks, 1993; Collins, Brown, & Newman, 1989; Marzano, 1992; and Spielberger, 1992.)

Constructivism proposes certain basic principles of learning:

1. Learning is not a passive receptive process, but is instead an active meaning-making process. It is the ability to perform complex cognitive tasks that require the active use and application of knowledge in solving meaningful problems.

2. Thus, learning at its best involves conceptual change—modifying one's previous understanding of concepts so that they are more complex and more valid. Typically the learner begins with a naive or inaccurate concept; the learning process enables the learner to develop a deeper or truer understanding of the concept.

3. In this sense, learning is always subjective and personal. The learner best learns when he or she can internalize what is being learned, representing it through learner-generated symbols, metaphors, images, graphics, and models.

4. Learning is also contextualized. Students carry out tasks and solve problems that resemble the nature of those tasks in the real world. Rather than doing "exercises" out of context, the students learn to solve contextualized problems.

5. Learning is social. Learning at its best involves interaction between learners, as meanings are shared, information is exchanged, and problems are solved cooperatively. In the process of solving problems, the learner interacts with others, learning from what they know and contributing to their knowledge.

Thus, knowledge is seen as shared and distributed—greater than the sum of its parts. The class in this sense becomes a social arena for examining knowledge, for testing what one knows, for increasing one's understanding.

6. Learning is affective. Thinking and feeling are closely related. The extent and nature of learning are influenced by the following affective elements: self-awareness and beliefs about one's abilities, clarity and strength of learning goals, personal expectations, general states of mind, and motivation to learn.

7. The nature of the learning task is crucial. The best learning tasks are characterized by these features: optimal difficulty, relevancy, authenticity, challenge, and novelty.

8. Learning is strongly influenced by the learner's development. Learners move through identifiable stages of physical, intellectual, emotional, and social growth that impact on what can be learned and in what depth of understanding. Learners seem to do best when the learning is at their proximal stage of development, challenging enough to require them to stretch, but attainable with effort.

9. Learning at its best involves metacognition, reflecting on one's learning throughout the entire learning process.

Constructivism seems to represent an excellent synthesis of the research on learning, one that is especially useful in teaching the academic subjects.

The Nature of Teacher Development

Knowing how teachers develop professionally can help principals in fostering continued growth. The following section begins with a review of what is known about adult learning in that teachers developing their skills should best be seen as adult learners. The next sections examine what is known about teachers' development, emphasizing their cognitive development, their level of motivation, and their stage of career development.

BOX 1.1

How Adults Learn:
A Synthesis of the Research

Structure of Learning Experiences

1. Prefer flexible schedules that respond to and take cognizance of their own time pressures
2. Learn better when learning is individualized—when they can pace their own learning, identify their own learning needs, and select their own learning experiences
3. Prefer face-to-face learning in classes, internships, and workshops; are less interested in audio and video cassettes and independent study
4. Derive benefit from heterogeneous classes in which they can interact with adults of different ages and with contrary views

Learning Climate

5. Seem to learn better in a climate characterized by mutual helpfulness and peer support
6. Are somewhat reluctant to take risks and therefore do better in a climate that is characterized by a sense of trust and acceptance of differences
7. Appreciate the opportunity to express views and are open to learning from those holding contrary opinions
8. Come to classes and workshops with clear expectations and hope that instructor will take their expectations into account in his or her planning for learning

Focus of Learning

9. Seem to derive the greatest benefit from teaching that helps them process their experience through reflection, analysis, and critical examination
10. Value learning that increases their autonomy and helps them create personal meaning
11. Interested in practical "how-to" learning that they can apply to immediate career-related issues

Teaching-Learning Strategies and Media

12. Value problem solving, cooperative learning
13. Desire active participation in the learning process, with constructive feedback; reluctant to sit through long lectures

---

Understanding How Adults Learn

Although adults vary a great deal in how they learn, the general findings summarized in Box 1.1 can be useful to principals as they think about supervising teachers. (The findings have been drawn

8 QUALITY TEACHING

chiefly from Cross, 1981; Knowles, 1984; and Lambert, 1984.) First, adults seem to prefer a learning structure that emphasizes flexibility of time and pacing, heterogeneity of group membership, individualization, and interaction with the instructor. Second, the learning climate is crucial to adults. They want to learn from each other and do better in a climate of trust, in which differing views are welcomed. They hold very clear expectations that they hope the instructor will take into account. They want the opportunity to process their experience and value practical learning that increases their autonomy. Finally, they value problem solving, cooperative learning, and active participation as learning processes.

Understanding Teachers' Cognitive Development

The teacher's cognitive development is usually equated with the extent to which the teacher can reason conceptually. Experts studying teachers' cognitive development usually identify three levels of abstract thinking—low, moderate, and high. Teachers at a low level think more concretely, differentiate fewer concepts, and tend to see problems simplistically; those at a high level can reason abstractly, see connections between diverse elements, and enjoy complexity. Several studies using the conceptual level as the focus have concluded the following about teachers at the high level (as contrasted with those at the low level): (a) they are more adaptable and flexible in teaching style, (b) they are more empathetic, (c) they provide more varied learning environments, (d) they are more tolerant of stress, (e) they are more effective with students of diverse ethnic backgrounds, and (f) they prefer to learn through a discovery model.

Although it would seem that one's cognitive level would be difficult to change, there is some evidence that cognitive development can be facilitated by making it possible for teachers to assume new roles (such as mentoring), as long as there is continuous guided reflection and ongoing support (Sprinthall & Thies-Sprinthall, 1983).

Understanding Teachers' Level of Motivation

Teachers vary considerably in their motivation to teach. Although they may be motivated to perform effectively in other areas (such as family or community life), too many teachers have lost their inner drive to excel as teachers. To help such teachers, principals should have a basic understanding of the factors that affect teacher motivation. These factors and their implications are more fully discussed in Chapter 7.

Even though some administrators mistakenly believe that teachers are motivated by higher salaries, the research presents a quite different picture. The factors that, according to the research, are likely to result in a higher level of motivation to teach are presented in the following (see Glatthorn, 1990, for further documentation).

A Supportive Environment for Quality Teaching. The school as a work environment can either foster teacher motivation or exercise a negative influence on it. The key aspects of a supportive environment for quality teaching are discussed more fully in Chapter 2.

Meaningful Work. The work of teaching is perceived as meaningful. The teacher perceives the work as challenging, with sufficient variety. The teacher believes that he or she is making a difference in students' lives and is convinced that teaching is fulfilling and meaningful. All adults seem to be driven to create meaning in their lives; effective teachers find that meaning chiefly in their teaching.

Belief System. The teacher believes in his or her sense of efficacy (the ability to make a difference) and is convinced that teaching actions will achieve the intended results. The teacher also believes that all students can learn, even though some can master some subjects better than others. Teachers who believe in their sense of efficacy and in students' potential go to school eager to teach.

Goals. The teacher's goals are shared by peers, they are specific (not too general), and they are attainable but challenging. The most powerful goals reflect what scholars call a *mastery orientation;* this mastery orientation emphasizes the value of hard work, taking on challenges, acquiring new skills, and making progress. Teachers who have clear goals and who see progress toward attaining those goals are more motivated than those who lack such support.

Rewards. Highly motivated teachers place more emphasis on such intrinsic rewards as a sense of competence and a feeling of accomplishment; student learning is perceived as a meaningful reward. Such teachers ask only for a salary that reflects their importance to the society; they are not motivated by merit pay.

Feedback. The teacher receives several kinds of feedback that indicate clearly that students are learning; the satisfaction that comes from seeing results is one of the strongest motivators. Teachers are also motivated by earned and timely praise from colleagues, supervisors, administrators, and returning students and graduates. Such feedback has high motivational potential.

Autonomy and Power. Teachers are more motivated when they have a large measure of control over the critical aspects of their work—what they teach, how they teach, how they assess student learning. Their belief that they have the power to make a difference leads them to take action and accept responsibility for their actions. Autonomy is especially important for experienced teachers; some novices are intimidated by the power they have.

Understanding Teachers' Career Development

The term *career development* is used here to mean the growth experienced as teachers move through the stages of their professional careers. Several researchers have investigated the patterns of growth and stagnation that emerge as teachers remain in the profession. One useful synthesis of the theory and research on career development results in five stages of the professional career, demarcated by years of teaching experience (Huberman, 1989).

Career entry, from the first to the third year, is a time of both survival and discovery. The survival theme is the one most often sounded in studies of beginning teachers. At the same time, many report a sense of discovery, as they work with their own pupils and become part of a collegial group. Most teachers at this stage of development prefer to receive assistance from a mentor who provides direct, on-site technical assistance.

Those with 4 to 6 years of teaching experience seem then to move into a *stabilization* period, when tenure is granted, a definitive commitment to the career of teaching is made, and a sense of instructional mastery is achieved. They are interested in trying new instructional approaches and developing more complex understanding of their students. The research suggests that they prefer to get assistance from experienced colleagues and need some technical help from supervisors.

Those with 7 to 18 years of experience seem to diverge. The best teachers report this period as one of *experimentation* and activism, when they try out new approaches, develop their own courses, and confront institutional barriers. Other teachers report this period as one of self-doubt and *reassessment,* when disenchantment with the system leads many to consider changing professions. Both groups seem to prefer nondirective, problem-solving supervision that helps them solve their own instructional problems, and they often turn to external sources (such as conferences and workshops) for assistance.

Divergence also occurs during the period of 19 to 30 years of experience. For many it is a time of relaxed *self-acceptance* and serenity, accompanied by a developing awareness of greater relational distance from their pupils. For many other teachers, this period is one of *conservatism;* these teachers seem to complain a great deal, criticizing their supervisors, their colleagues, and their students. Both groups are interested in self-directed approaches to professional growth and want the opportunity to design their own staff development programs.

The final period, 31 to 40 years of teaching experience, is a stage of *disengagement,* a gradual withdrawal as the end of the career looms. For some it is a time of serenity; for others, a time of bitterness. The withdrawal seems to move their minds away from professional growth and toward retirement; supervision is usually perceived as an unwanted intrusion. (More detail about these stages and supervisory needs can be found in Burden, 1982; and Christensen, Burke, Fessler, & Hagstrom, 1983.)

Both teachers and principals should realize that these stages are only very tentative categories for describing teachers in general, not rigid boxes into which all teachers should be placed. For example, many beginning teachers exhibit the characteristics of those at the second stage; many teachers close to retirement are still pushing themselves toward further growth. In the best of schools, the stages are less important: All teachers, regardless of the length of their experience, are pushing ahead to new growth.

The Implications for Principals

What do the foregoing analyses mean for principals? Several implications seem important, both for working with all teachers and for providing for individualized services to special groups of teachers.

Working With All Teachers

The principal should emphasize to all teachers that the ultimate goal is quality learning for all students—and that quality teaching is the best way to achieve that ultimate goal. To achieve that goal of quality teaching, the principal should ensure that certain approaches and supports are provided for all teachers (these are explained in Chapter 2). Then, as the principal plans for and implements staff development programs to promote quality teaching, he or she should apply the research on adult learning, keeping in mind that they are working with adults, not young learners. Next, by making both informal and more systematic observations of classrooms, the principal should make a tentative determination of the skill level of each teacher, in that such information would be important to the principal in deciding how to individualize supervision.

Individualizing Supervision for Groups of Teachers

As explained above, teachers vary in many other significant ways— in their level of motivation, in their moral development, in the phase of the life cycle in which they find themselves, and, most important of all, in their ability to teach. Although it is important to see teachers as individuals, this book identifies four major types of teachers (listed in Table 1.2), factoring in career development, cognitive development, teaching competence, and motivation to teach.

TABLE 1.2 Typology for Supervisory Services

Type/Factor	Career Stage	Cognitive Level	Competence Level	Motivation Level
Novices	Career entry	Mixed	Working on basic skills	Generally high
Marginal	Stabilization, reassessment	Generally low	Have not mastered basic skills	Generally low
Passive	Reassessment, conservatism	Mixed	Mixed; most have mastered basic skills	Very low
Productive	Experimentation, self-acceptance	High	Intermediate or advanced	High

Novice teachers are those at the first stage of career development, usually high in motivation and low in expertise, functioning at the basic level. *Marginal* teachers are those at the second and third stages in career development, low in motivation and still struggling to master several of the fundamental skills of teaching. *Passive* teachers are those who have lost their motivation to teach; they are passive in their attitudes toward school improvement, in their approach to teaching, and in the kind of learning they provide. The passive group includes teachers at advanced levels of career development, who have mastered the basic skills, but who have lost their motivation to teach and are not interested in moving to a higher level of skill development. Finally, *productive* teachers are those who are competent and continue to grow; the group includes teachers at the intermediate level of skill development and expert teachers functioning at an advanced level. They are high in both motivation and competence, the core of each productive faculty.

Chapter 2 explains how to provide a supportive environment for all teachers. Chapter 3 suggests how the principal can organize for the effective delivery of such individualized services. Chapters 4, 5, 6, and

7 offer specific recommendations for working with the four groups of teachers. Chapter 8 focuses on the needs of the nonteaching staff. The final chapter explains how to secure the special resources needed.

Most of all, however, principals should remember that teachers are professional individuals. No generalization or classification system, no matter how much it is supported by research, can ever take the place of sensitivity to the needs and strengths of individual teachers.

Developing the Learning Community

Although the central argument of this book is that principals should individualize the supervisory services provided to teachers, they should also ensure that certain conditions and services are available to all teachers, regardless of experience, motivation, and skill. Those essential conditions and services are presented here as the components of a *learning community*.

As conceptualized here, that learning community is pervasively influenced by a learning-centered culture, which manifests itself in certain basic values and their related norms. The learning community rests on critically important foundations—the basics that must be present if the school is to be a center for learning. That culture and those foundations are actualized through appropriate structures for involvement and development. Those structures in turn are operationalized in three ways: through facilitating work conditions, effective services, and professional relationships. The entire set of components is set in place and made effective through learning-centered leadership. Figure 2.1 presents a conceptual framework for the learning

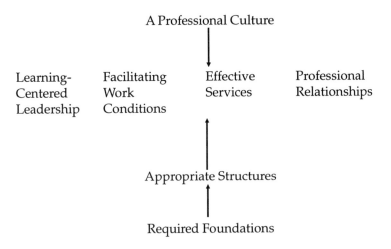

Figure 2.1. Components of the Learning Community

community; each component is discussed in the following sections. (The framework is drawn from Blase & Kirby, 1992; Conley & Cooper, 1991; Corcoran, 1990; Duttweiler, 1988; Johnson, 1990; Louis, 1992; Maehr, Smith, & Midgley, 1990; Rosenholtz, 1989; Scott & Smith, 1987; and Sergiovanni, 1994.)

A Professional Culture

Culture refers to the shared values of the organization's members that give rise to shared norms of behavior. Four values and their associated norms seem to be crucial; they are presented here as slogans that might greet visitors to the school.

The first is "Learning for All Is Our Central Mission." All members of the organization have internalized the school's mission, have in common a vision of excellence for that school, and work toward shared goals. Obviously, student learning is the first priority. All the major decisions are made on the basis of their contribution to student learning. However, the learning of teachers and administrators is also considered to be important. Thus, the school structures itself as a center for inquiry, where teachers and principals work together in the pursuit of their own professional development. Everyone in the school is expected to be engaged in the continuing processes of inquiring, studying, and reflecting.

The second value is "Collegiality and Cooperation Foster Continued Improvement." Teachers and administrators see themselves as partners in a shared enterprise, collaborating with students and parents to improve the school. Teachers collaborate with each other in a variety of ways: producing materials, giving each other feedback, conducting action research, and engaging in professional dialogue. That collaboration is goal oriented, aimed at solving emerging problems in the school's quest for continuing improvement. Cooperation is expected of all participants in the learning enterprise as they work toward achieving their goals.

The third value is "Teaching Is a Profession That Deserves Respect." Rather than being viewed as assembly line workers producing human products, teachers are regarded as members of an honored profession, given the recognition and respect they deserve. As staff development is planned and supervision is carried out, principals treat teachers as professionals, trusting them to define their own needs and assume responsibility for their own growth. Teachers are viewed as professional decision makers, intentionally reshaping the learning environment so that it is more supportive for all.

The final value is "We Value Accomplishment and Recognize Productivity." As determined by researchers, a school that values goal accomplishment and recognizes productivity increases teachers' commitment to that organization and to the profession of teaching (Maehr et al., 1990). This task orientation, as they determined, is more important than a sense of affiliation or the concern for personal relationships. They note, however, that this emphasis on accomplishment and recognition must be couched in noncompetitive terms.

The Required Foundations

The required foundations may be seen as the minimum essentials that must be present if teachers are to function effectively. Three components are critical. First, teachers should be paid salaries that reflect their importance to the society. Even though teacher salaries are beyond the control of the principal, principals should be aware of their importance as a foundation for a supportive work environment. Second, teachers should feel that they are in a safe, orderly, and comfortable physical environment. The prevalence of violence in the schools—much of it directed at teachers—makes safety the most important of all. Finally, adequate resources should be provided for teachers to do a quality job: They should have the textbooks, computers, and other instructional materials required for student learning.

The Appropriate Structures

The appropriate structures are the policies and procedures, and the committees and task forces that are needed to ensure the effective operation of the schools. Two types of structures are considered important: structures for development and structures for involvement. The structures for development are those needed to ensure the continued professional development of all personnel (they are fully discussed in Chapter 3).

The structures for involvement are those needed to provide the means for the effective involvement of teachers in decision making. Each school, of course, will have its own structures. The following types are considered essential.

Instructional Teams. Instructional teams are the basic structure for both teaching and decision making. As noted in later chapters, the instructional team will also be useful as the locus of professional development. Elementary and middle schools will probably organize teams by grade level; high schools, by departments or interdepartmental teams. As McLaughlin (1994) notes, the team or department is the natural location for teachers to reflect about their teaching, collaborate on instructional projects, and learn together.

The Central Decision-Making Body. The principal and the teachers need to establish a leadership team that will use input from the faculty and their own knowledge and experience to identify problems, appoint special task forces, and make critical decisions. In some schools, this is identified as the principal's cabinet; in others, the school improvement team. The name is not important, but the function is. The group will be composed largely of teachers—some schools include all the leaders of the instructional teams.

Special Task Forces. Once a major problem has been identified, the central group should appoint a task force with the specific responsibility of studying the problem and developing proposed solutions, which in turn are reviewed by the central group before being presented to the faculty. The task force is the chief means by which interdepartmental or cross-team issues are addressed.

Faculty Meetings. Faculty meetings should be devoted to only two purposes: professional development and problem identification and solution. These meetings can be effective means for bringing teachers up to date on current research and helping them examine current issues. They also are the best means for identifying problems and reviewing the solutions proposed by the task forces. In leading these meetings, the principal should avoid premature vote taking, which only increases divisiveness. Instead, the principal should use the meeting as an opportunity for building consensus among the faculty.

These structures for involvement will give every teacher an opportunity to participate actively in decision making, without burdening teachers with administrative responsibilities they do not wish to assume.

Facilitating Work Conditions

There are several work conditions that should be found in every professional work environment. First, quality time should be provided for teachers to plan, produce materials, carry out action research, and give each other feedback. This quality time is especially critical if collaboration is to take place. Often when teachers have been invited to participate in peer coaching, they resist because collegiality takes time, a scarce commodity in schools.

Also, teachers' work should be structured so that it is meaningful. They should have appropriate autonomy with respect to curriculum, instruction, and student evaluation. If teachers lack autonomy in these vital areas, they will tend to feel that they are similar to assembly line workers, simply operationalizing what others have decided.

Teachers also need teachable assignments: They should teach subjects in their own areas of expertise and not have more than two preparations. They should have a room of their own, if at all possible, and should have classes that are not exceptionally difficult to instruct.

Finally, mechanisms should be in place for teachers to receive useful feedback. They should receive and be helped to use student achievement results. They should get timely and merited praise from supervisors and administrators. And they should receive constructive feedback about their teaching from students, colleagues, supervisors, and administrators.

Effective Services

All teachers need several types of supportive services from the principal. First, they should receive frequent informal visits from the principal. Such informal observations need to last only 5 to 10 minutes. The principal drops in, makes an initial scan of the learning processes at work, noting how many students seem on task, and then observes what the teacher is doing to facilitate learning. Many principals have found that a "no-carbon-required" form is useful in giving the teacher prompt feedback. It looks similar to the form shown in Box 2.1.

These informal observations serve many purposes. Most important, they give the principal an opportunity to give the teacher specific, timely, and merited praise. They enable the principal to make an informal assessment of curriculum implementation. They also keep the principal highly visible, a principal behavior that teachers value. Finally, the informal reports also serve as a "distant early warning" system of problems that are just emerging. For example, if the principal makes three informal observations and notes that on each occasion the teacher has been seated at the desk while students complete drill-and-practice sheets, a conference would obviously be needed. These observations, however, should not be used in the formal teacher evaluation system in that they are brief and unstructured.

The informal observations are so essential that principals should put aside a block of time each day for such purposes. How much time

---

BOX 2.1

Informal Observation Form

On *December 10* I briefly visited your *math* class.
I liked *the way small groups were solving a*
meaningful problem.
I had a question about *why two boys were working*
at the back of the room on their own;
they did not seem engaged in the task.

Date: *December 10*   Signature:

---

is reserved will depend, of course, on the size of the faculty—in most schools, one hour a day would be sufficient. At the end of one week, a principal who has set aside one hour a day would have observed at least 20 teachers.

The second type of developmental service all teachers need is effective *staff development.* The term is used here to denote organized learning experiences for groups of teachers. The most effective staff development programs are (a) planned by the principal and teachers, with the principal actively participating but not dominating, (b) focused on school improvement, (c) linked with teacher supervision, (d) supported with peer coaching, (e) organized to be ongoing and systematic (not "one-shot" sessions), (f) ones emphasizing active learning, and (g) evaluated carefully. (For the research on staff development, see Glatthorn, 1990.)

Next, all teachers need structured opportunities to meet with the principal—to exchange ideas, to identify emerging concerns, to share views of current issues. Principals can satisfy this need in several ways: by meeting periodically with teams and departments; by holding informal seminars before school, during lunch, and during teachers' unscheduled time; and by reserving a portion of each faculty meeting for such exchanges.

Finally, the principal should keep in mind the importance of using routine as a means of strengthening professional relationships. As Leithwood (1992) observes, effective principals accept the fragmented nature of their role and use many informal and seemingly routine interactions to emphasize everyday factors that impinge on learning.

Thus, a principal monitoring students as they move though the corridors between periods can stop to talk briefly with a teacher about the importance of corridor traffic as a site for potential disruption.

Professional Relationships

The climate of the learning community is characterized by positive relationships between the teachers and the principal, the students and the teachers, and parents and the school. Positive relationships involve certain critical elements such as the following: there is mutual respect for each other, participants work together without excessive friction, there is a spirit of inclusiveness that militates against the negative effects of cliques, and the participants are open in their praise of each other. Such positive relationships in the school have a major impact on the morale of all involved. Byrne (1994) determined that student-teacher relationships (as manifested in a positive classroom climate) and peer relationships were critical elements in reducing teacher burnout.

Note, however, that the presence of positive relationships does not mean the absence of conflict. Instead, conflict is dealt with constructively. When conflict inevitably develops between the principal and the teachers, they should be sure to let conflict surface and deal with it constructively, solving problems, not fixing blame. When conflict develops between the teacher and the student that cannot be resolved at the classroom level or between the teacher and the parents, the teacher needs the support of the principal.

Learning-Centered Leadership

The school as a learning community is led by a principal who keeps the central mission of the school in the forefront and takes the needed actions to accomplish that mission. The complex issue here is for the principal to empower teachers through team leadership without abdicating the principal's authority. Studies of effective principals indicate that they have found ways of increasing teacher power while at the same time maintaining their role as instructional leader. While the principal works with a leadership team and a central decision-making body, the principal maintains an active role as instructional leader.

The research suggests that the following principal behaviors are vital in executing such a role (the following summary draws from Blase & Kirby, 1992; Cunningham & Gresso, 1993; Lee, 1987; Sergiovanni, 1992; Smith & Andrews, 1989):

- Actively shapes the school culture so that it embodies and supports learning-centered values
- Discerns and articulates a vision of excellence and enables others to share effectively in the visioning process
- Is aware of the moral dimensions of schooling, acts ethically, and sensitizes teachers and students to the moral aspects of teaching and learning
- Maintains a focus on curriculum and instruction, by informing teachers of current developments, sharing knowledge gained from experience, observing teachers at work, monitoring the implementation of the curriculum, and rewarding effective teaching
- Uses routine activities and informal interactions as means of reinforcing the teachers' commitment to learning
- Uses persuasion and influence to improve the quality of learning, while using formal authority as needed
- Creates a climate of high expectations for all, while providing the support needed to realize such expectations: assists teachers in acquiring new skills, supports teachers in disciplinary matters, builds a school curriculum that is developmentally appropriate
- Secures additional resources and allocates resources in a manner that best accomplishes organizational goals: defends instructional time, mobilizes special personnel as needed, builds a learning-centered schedule
- Uses a problem-solving approach in fostering continuing improvement: evaluates formatively and summatively, investigates problems, uses reflection to gain insight into problems, uses structures that enable others to become involved in the problem-solving process

- Provides services and structures to the entire faculty and to individuals that foster their professional growth
- Communicates effectively, giving earned and timely praise to all who merit it
- Ensures a school climate that is safe, orderly, and learning focused
- Actively involves parents to enlist their support, to aid them in providing a supportive learning environment, and to use their insights and talents in improving the schools

The schoolwide elements discussed above provide a sound foundation for the developmental structures and individualized assistance discussed in the succeeding chapters.

Effective Delivery
of Supervisory Services

How can the principal organize the faculty for the effective delivery of differentiated services to develop individual teachers? There is no single best answer. The optimal response will vary depending on several factors: (a) school district policies, (b) the size of the district and the school, (c) the principal's style of leadership, (d) the administrative and supervisory staffing, (e) the level of schooling (elementary, middle, or high), (f) the size of the school, and (g) the composition of the faculty. Rather than recommending a single organizational pattern, this chapter presents some basic principles to keep in mind in organizing for supervision, reviews the options available in designing programs, and explains a process principals can use in designing their own organizational system.

Organizing for Effective Supervision

In developing an organizational system for supervision, principals and teachers should keep in mind some basic principles. The basic

---

BOX 3.1

Basic Principles in Organizing for Supervision

The Goals

1. The ultimate goal is quality learning. All supervisory services should focus on producing quality learning through quality teaching.
2. A related goal is school improvement. The program should relate teacher development to school improvement as a means of creating a synergistic relationship.

The Constraints

3. All supervisory programs must conform with state regulations, district policies, and the provisions of the teachers' contract.

The School Culture

4. All programs should be built upon a strong professional culture—one that values learning for all, collegiality and cooperation, continuous improvement, the professionalism of teaching, and the importance of shared vision and goals.

Authority

5. The superintendent has final authority about the design and operation of the program: In that the principal is primarily accountable for the success of the school, the superintendent should delegate that authority to the principal.
6. In that teachers are primarily affected by the supervision program, they should have maximum input into its design.

General Features

7. All programs should make a clear distinction between *development* (those services provided to help teachers improve) and *evaluation* (those services designed to evaluate performance for the purposes of administrative decision making).

---

principles shown in Box 3.1 have been derived from research on effective programs and reports of exemplary practice (e.g., see Glatthorn, 1990; Hargreaves, 1992; Loucks-Horsley et al., 1987; McLaughlin & Pfeifer, 1988; Stiggins & Duke, 1988).

The Goals

The principal needs to remind other administrators, supervisors, and teachers that the goal is quality learning. Although this goal might seem obvious, the reality is that too many professionals who provide supervisory services get caught up in a mindless implementation of

---

BOX 3.1

(Continued)

8. In that teachers vary in their ability and needs, all development programs should make adequate provisions for those individual differences.

9. In that many teachers experience significant changes over the course of the year, programs should provide for flexibility in the types of developmental services provided.

10. The program should not stigmatize any individual teacher or group of teachers but should instead recognize the growth potential of all.

11. No program should be so complex or bureaucratic that it consumes inordinate amounts of the principal's and teachers' time.

12. All services should be based on and provide for reflection, the process of recalling and making sense of past experience.

13. All programs should respect the teacher as a knowledgeable professional; the teacher should be seen as the expert with respect to his or her classroom.

Requirements for All Teachers

14. The program should mandate the participation of all teachers in district- and school-organized staff development programs.

15. All programs should respect the right of the principal to have full access to all classrooms; thus, the performance of all teachers will be monitored, regardless of what other services are provided.

Resources

16. All programs should be supported with adequate resources, especially quality time.

---

procedures and lose sight of the learning process. As they observe classes, they focus unduly on teaching methods, ignoring the central issue of whether students are learning. With this focus on learning, the principal should also cooperate with the teachers in designing programs that link teacher development to school improvement. Thus, the concern is not primarily how to help a few weak teachers become better; instead the central question is how to make the school a more effective organization—through quality teaching by the entire faculty.

The Constraints

Every program needs to recognize the limits imposed by state regulations, district policies with respect to teacher supervision and evaluation, and the provisions of the teacher contract that relate to those areas. One of the early steps in the process to be explained in a later section is analyzing those constraints to ensure that the program developed does not ignore those limits.

The School Culture

The importance of the culture needs to be emphasized here again. If the elements of a strong culture identified in Chapter 2 are present, then effective supervision seems to flourish without undue attention. If those elements are absent, then even those programs that have been effective elsewhere experience serious difficulty. A case in point is the use of peers in supervision and planning. As one scholar has noted, if peer coaching and team planning are implemented from above in a culture that does not value cooperation, the result is what he called "contrived collegiality," a superficial and ineffective use of peers in a team relationship (Hargreaves, 1992).

Authority

Effective programs balance the formal authority of the principal as delegated by the superintendent, and the power of the teachers as expressed through their group and individual decision making. In designing the program, the principal and teachers need to work together as active collaborators; in implementing the program, the principal should be sensitive to teacher concerns but should have final authority about how teachers will be supervised and evaluated.

General Features

Several of the general features noted require a more detailed explication. First, all programs should distinguish between two separate functions. *Development* (often termed *supervision*) refers to the supportive services provided to teachers to foster their professional growth. *Evaluation* is used in a somewhat restricted sense to mean the process of giving teachers ratings (such as *satisfactory* or *unsatisfactory*) for purposes of administrative decision making (to grant or deny tenure, to renew or not renew the contract, to promote or not promote). Although most districts claim that their evaluation programs are intended to improve instruction, there is no evidence that they do, as Glickman (1991) points out. Fair and objective evaluations are needed to make wise personnel decisions, but they have little to do with improving teachers' performance.

The principles also call for programs that are individualized, flexible, professional, and relatively simple. An individualized program will respond to the differences among teachers in their needs and preferences by offering them several optional approaches. A flexible program will enable the principal in consultation with the teacher to change at any time the developmental approaches used with the teacher. A professional program does not embarrass or stigmatize the teacher, even the incompetent. As explained later, some teachers will need intensive help, but that decision should be made in a manner that respects the teacher's professionalism and need for privacy. The best programs will also be relatively simple for both administrators and teachers to implement. When so-called performance objectives programs for evaluating teachers were implemented, both principals and teachers complained vociferously about the inordinate amount of paperwork entailed.

All the services provided should emphasize reflection, the process of recalling and making personal sense of significant experiences. Supervisory conferences should help the teacher solve learning problems by analyzing the observational data and reflecting about likely causes and effective solutions to classroom-based problems. Finally, the program should be based on a respect for the teacher as a knowledgeable professional. Those involved in implementing the program should view the teacher as an expert about his or her students and classroom. In too many instances, supervisors see themselves as experts, advising the teacher about what should be done.

Requirements for All Teachers

Although the program should provide options for teachers, certain requirements should apply to all. First, as noted in Chapter 2, all teachers, regardless of their expertise, would be required to participate in district- and school-sponsored staff development programs. Also, the principal should monitor all classrooms, making brief informal

observations or "drop-in" visits to observe and reinforce good teaching, to assess general school climate, and to note the presence of any
emerging teaching and learning problems.

Resources

All programs should provide adequate resources for teacher development—funds, trained personnel, and quality time. That last
resource is especially crucial. Many teachers prefer to work on their
own, simply because peer involvement is too time-consuming. And
teachers will not learn very much from staff development programs
held at the end of the school day.

Program Options

In designing their own program, principals and teachers should
be aware of the options available to them. The following discussion
examines the basic structures and specific strategies that can be used
both in teacher evaluation and teacher development. The term *basic
structure* is used here to mean a special evaluation or developmental
program, such as "intensive evaluation" or "cooperative development." The term *specific strategy* is used to designate particular processes to be used, such as an evaluative observation or peer coaching.

Options for Teacher Evaluation

Although this book is not centrally concerned with teacher evaluation, the evaluation process is clearly related to teacher development
and thus needs to be understood by program designers. In determining the basic structures for an evaluation program, three choices are
available to administrators and teachers.

Intensive Evaluation. Intensive evaluation denotes an intensive
process used to make administrative decisions regarding certification,
tenure, contract renewal, or promotion. This type of evaluation is
usually provided to novice teachers (including teachers new to that
building until they have demonstrated their competence), marginal

teachers (tenured teachers who are judged as marginal performers), and passive teachers (unmotivated teachers who have shown no desire to improve). It usually is implemented by an administrator who has had special training in evaluation; in some school systems, an external evaluator is used. Intensive evaluation involves rigorous assessment employing all of the following strategies:

- The taking-stock conference is held to assess performance to that date. Usually it is held three times a year: at the beginning of the year (to set the evaluation agenda), at the end of the first term (to assess progress), and toward the end of the school year (to make and report a summative evaluation).
- Evaluative observations use a standard form that specifies the criteria to be used and the indicators to be observed. The following is an example:

    CRITERION: Uses time effectively.

    INDICATORS: Begins class promptly; maximizes instructional time; uses routines to gain efficiency; handles transitions effectively; avoids wasting time at end of class period.

    Most experts in the field recommend that a minimum of 5 evaluative observations be made.
- Evaluative conferences are usually held after each evaluative observation and are intended to supplement the taking-stock conferences.
- Anecdotal reports of performance of noninstructional duties are made if the administrator observes excellent performance, unsatisfactory performance, or nonperformance of such duties.
- A special conference is held to evaluate teacher planning, in which the evaluator assesses yearly plans, unit plans, and daily lesson plans.
- Evaluation of student assessment and record keeping (which may be combined with the planning conference) examines a test the teacher plans to give, one the teacher has given and graded, the teacher's roll book, and student performance on curriculum-referenced tests.

The information from these sources is synthesized into a summative evaluation, typically using the terms *satisfactory, unsatisfactory,* and *more than satisfactory* and delivered in the final taking-stock conference.

Obviously, intensive evaluation, as the term implies, is a rigorous and demanding process that will require a significant time commitment from the principal. If the principal has a large number of teachers on the intensive evaluation track, the principal can reduce the number to be evaluated, secure additional assistance, or simplify the process by reducing the length and number of observations.

Standard Evaluation. Standard evaluation designates the basic evaluation structure used in assessing the productive teachers. The evaluator makes the minimum number of evaluative observations specified by policies and contracts (usually two each year) and holds one end-of-year taking-stock conference. This type of evaluation is a routine one, primarily used to comply with regulations.

Evaluation for Development. Evaluation for development designates the evaluation structure that is essentially concerned with teacher development but is termed *evaluation* chiefly to comply with state or district requirements. Typically it would be provided for productive teachers, but it may also include the passive. In most such programs, the teacher, in consultation with the principal, sets one or two goals for the year in a taking-stock conference, works toward accomplishing those goals, and meets with the principal in an end-of-year taking-stock conference to assess achievement and identify future goals. The strategies used by the teacher in accomplishing the goals are discussed later in this chapter. This type of evaluation should not be used as the basis for administrative decision making in that it is not sufficiently standardized or rigorous for such purposes.

Most schools will find that intensive evaluation and evaluation for development are sufficient to accommodate the needs of all teachers, without requiring inordinate amounts of time from principals and teachers.

Table 3.1 summarizes the basic structures of evaluation with respect to the four groups of teachers. Principals should remember that these are only recommendations, to be interpreted and implemented flexibly.

TABLE 3.1 Evaluation Structures and Teacher Groups

| | *Evaluation Structures* | | |
Teachers	*Intensive*	*Standard*	*Evaluation for Development*
Novices	Yes	No	No
Marginal	Yes	No	No
Passive	Maybe	Maybe	Maybe
Productive	No	Maybe	Maybe

Options for Teacher Development

Three basic developmental structures are available to the principal and the teachers.

Intensive Development. Intensive development, usually termed *clinical supervision,* is provided to the teachers assigned to intensive evaluation—novices, marginal, and passive. It typically uses five required strategies and one or more optional strategies. The required strategies are as follows.

- The taking-stock conference, again, is usually held three times: once at the start of the year, at the end of the first semester, and at the end of the year. The conference gives the teacher and the supervisor an opportunity to make general assessments of progress.
- Diagnostic observations are used to identify general strengths and specific needs. Typically, four or more would be made throughout the year, with an optional preobservation conference.
- A diagnostic conference would be held after each diagnostic observation, after the supervisor has had an opportunity to analyze the observational data.
- The diagnostic observation, analysis, and conference would identify one skill requiring development. The supervisor would then provide some intensive coaching in that skill to provide a rationale, explain the steps, demonstrate, provide for guided

practice with feedback, and structure independent practice with feedback.

- A focused observation is made to collect data with respect to the skill that was coached and then shared in a conference.

In addition to these required strategies, the supervisor and teacher may decide to use one or more of the following optional strategies:

- Journal keeping (the teacher records significant actions and reflects about his or her experiences and reading)
- Professional study (includes graduate courses and systematic reading of professional books and journals)
- Curriculum development (involves the development of instructional units)
- Learning materials development (involves the production of student learning materials designed to supplement or replace the text)
- Videotape analysis (includes the analysis of a videotape of one of the teacher's classes, with the supervisor assisting in the analysis)

As explained in later chapters, intensive development is usually provided by a mentor. Regardless of who provides the service, the process is labor-intensive, requiring the commitment of large amounts of time. If there are large numbers of teachers on the intensive development track, the principal may decide to simplify the process by reducing the number and length of observations.

Self-Directed Development. Self-directed development enables individual teachers to work on their own, focusing on one or more professional growth goals. (As noted earlier, it is termed *evaluation for development,* when used to comply with evaluation policies.) Ordinarily, self-directed development is recommended only for productive teachers. It empowers such teachers to explore special areas of interest. One teacher we know became so interested in the concept of teacher efficacy that she wrote a book about it; another teacher became intrigued with learning styles and began writing and publishing a newspaper column on the topic and related educational issues.

It is usually not offered to novices and marginal teachers, in that it does not provide sufficient coaching and feedback. And it typically is not made available to the passive, because it requires a great deal of autonomy and self-motivation to succeed.

Self-directed development has only one requirement: that the principal and teacher hold two stock-taking conferences, one at the beginning of the year (to identify the developmental goal) and one at the end (to assess progress and examine future goals). Any of the optional strategies noted above may be used, depending on the goal identified. Also, the teacher working in the self-directed mode may use any of the strategies required for intensive development.

Cooperative Development. Cooperative development involves groups of peers working together for their professional growth. Typically, groups are from 3 to 10 in number. They may be based on existing instructional groups (such as grade-level teams or subject-departments) or are organized separately for the purposes of development. Cooperative development is strongly recommended for all teachers; novices and marginal teachers should participate in cooperative groups as a supplement to their intensive development. It seems especially valuable for both passive and productive teachers.

Again, two stock-taking conferences are usually required—one at the beginning and one at the end of the year. Depending on the goal identified and the team's preferences, one or more of the following strategies may be used (note again that those working in cooperative development may choose from any of the strategies identified for intensive or self-directed):

- Professional dialogues (structured discussions of issues and related readings)
- Curriculum development
- Learning materials development
- Action research (in which the team members identify, study, and solve a school-related problem)

TABLE 3.2 Teachers and Developmental Structures

| | Developmental Structures | | |
Teachers	Intensive	Self-Directed	Cooperative
Novices	Required	Not recommended	Recommended
Marginal	Required	Not recommended	Recommended
Passive	Optional	Not recommended	Recommended
Productive	Not recommended	Recommended	Recommended

- Peer coaching (in which members of the team observe each other and then hold peer-directed conferences)

Table 3.2 summarizes the groups of teachers and the basic developmental structures available to them. Table 3.3 shows the specific strategies available for each structure and whether they are required, recommended, or optional. The required strategies are those essential for a given structure to operate effectively; the recommended strategies are those strongly supported by the research; the optional ones would be potentially useful.

A Recommended Process
for Developing a System

The process begins with the appointment of a task force, which will submit recommendations to the school's decision-making body. The task force first analyzes the constraints that will be operative in designing the program to be sure that the final program lives within the limits imposed by the constraints.

The task force then proceeds to address the issues listed in Box 3.2, reviewing the research, examining reports of exemplary practice, and

TABLE 3.3 Developmental Structures and Strategies

	Structures		
Strategies	*Intensive*	*Self-Directed*	*Cooperative*
Taking-stock conference	Required	Required	Required
Diagnostic observation (with optional preobservation conference)	Required	Optional	Optional
Diagnostic conference	Required	Optional	Optional
Coaching by supervisor	Required	Optional	Optional
Peer coaching	Optional	Optional	Recommended
Focused observation	Required	Recommended	Optional
Journal keeping	Optional	Optional	Optional
Professional study	Optional	Optional	Optional
Curriculum development	Optional	Optional	Recommended
Learning materials development	Optional	Optional	Recommended
Videotape analysis	Optional	Recommended	Recommended
Professional dialogues	Optional	Optional	Optional
Action research	Optional	Optional	Recommended

BOX 3.2

Issues to Resolve in Program Design

Constraints

1. What constraints exist in state regulations, board policies, administrative regulations, and teacher contract? Will an exemption from any of these constraints be requested?

Teacher Evaluation

2. What basic structure will be used in designing the evaluation program: (a) separate tracks will be used depending on tenure status and competence; (b) all teachers will experience the same evaluation each year; or (c) teachers will be organized into cohorts, with one cohort evaluated each year?
3. If separate tracks are used, who will be primarily responsible for administering each track?
4. If separate tracks are used, what processes will be used for each?
5. If separate tracks are used, what processes will be used to assign teachers to a given track? How and when may a teacher move from one track to another?
6. If all teachers will experience the same evaluation each year, who will be responsible for administering the program, and what will be its chief features?
7. If cohorts will be used, how will they be established?

Teacher Development

8. Will all teachers experience the same basic structure of developmental assistance, or will a variety of structures be used?
9. If all teachers experience the same type, who will be responsible for providing developmental services?

---

analyzing the special needs of the school. The discussion that follows examines those design issues that need special attention.

The task force should first turn its attention to the evaluation issues, in that those are the ones most often constrained by external policy-making groups. Two patterns of differentiated evaluation programs are found in practice: the *cohort* program and the *competence* program. Typically, in the cohort program, the faculty are divided into four (and sometimes, three) cohorts; cohorts may be established randomly, by teacher preference, or by instructional team. During the first year, Cohort 1 experiences intensive evaluation; the remaining cohorts, standard evaluation or evaluation for development. During the second year, Cohort 2 is in intensive evaluation, with Cohorts 1, 3, and 4 in the alternative modes. And thus the cycle continues for 4 years.

BOX 3.2

(Continued)

10. If all teachers experience the same type, what will be its general features?

11. If separate tracks are to be used, how will teachers be assigned to a particular track? How and when may they move from one track to another?

12. If separate tracks are to be used, who will be responsible for administering each track?

13. If separate tracks are to be used, what will be the chief features of each?

14. If some form of cooperative development is to be used, how will groups be structured?

Relationships of Components

15. Will information gathered through development activities be available to evaluators? If so, how and under what conditions?

16. Will information gathered through evaluation be available to those responsible for development? If so, how and under what conditions?

17. Will information gathered through classroom monitoring be used by evaluators or supervisors? If so, how and under what conditions?

18. How will staff development programs be related to teacher evaluation and development?

Program Evaluation

19. How often will the program be evaluated?

20. Who will be responsible for designing and implementing the program evaluation?

Those advocating the cohort approach point out that it ensures that all teachers will experience a rigorous evaluation on a periodic basis.

In the competence program, all novices are assigned to intensive evaluation, until they have demonstrated mastery of the basic skills. Marginal teachers who have proved to be deficient in one or more of the basic skills are also assigned to the intensive track, again until they have demonstrated comprehensive mastery. The principal determines whether a passive teacher would do better in the intensive evaluation group or in one of the options. Productive teachers are evaluated with the standard or developmental approach.

The task force should then turn its attention to the developmental structures, ensuring that they complement the evaluation choices. Ordinarily, all those assigned to intensive evaluation are also assigned to intensive development until they have demonstrated basic compe-

TABLE 3.4 Sample Program

| | Programs | |
Teacher Group	Evaluation	Development
Novice	Intensive	Intensive, along with cooperative instructional teams
Marginal	Intensive	Intensive, along with cooperative instructional teams
Passive	Evaluation for development	Cooperative instructional teams
Productive	Standard	Cooperative instructional teams

tence. Note, however, that those assigned to intensive development may also volunteer to participate in the self-directed or cooperative mode. The important matter here is to ensure that they are receiving the intensive assistance they need.

For the rest of the teachers, the task force has several options, as follows.

First, they may decide that all remaining teachers will work in a self-directed mode. Second, they may decide that all remaining teachers will work in a cooperative mode. Third, they may decide that the rest of the teachers will not participate in any structured developmental program, other than staff development and informal observations. Or, finally, they may decide to let all the remaining teachers express a preference, with the principal making the final decision in conference with each teacher.

A special note should be made here as to the nature of the cooperative groups. Here the task force has two choices. First, they may decide to base the cooperative groups on the instructional teams already in operation. Thus, in an elementary school, all the fifth grade teachers would constitute one cooperative group; in this manner the instructional team is chiefly responsible for the professional development of its own members. Or they may decide to set up cooperative

groups based on the teachers' preferences. Thus, a high school cooperative group might include one teacher from each department. Although the second option has the advantage of bringing together
teachers with disparate assignments, the instructional team option
seems to have greater power for making a significant difference and
takes less time in that it can use team planning periods.

Although these matters may make program design seem almost too
complicated to bother with, the task force can design a high-quality
homegrown program, if they take the time to review the research, the
recommendations in this book, and the reports of other schools. Table
3.4 provides one simple design that has worked successfully in several
schools.

Supporting Productive Teachers

Portrait of Marilyn Williamson

Marilyn Williamson teaches third grade. She is 45 years old and has been teaching for 23 years. She holds a master's degree in supervision but is not interested in a supervisory position: She just likes to teach.

Although Marilyn never discusses family problems with her friends on the faculty, she has let Principal Georgio know that she is going through some stressful times. She and her husband of 20 years are separating, her 15-year-old son has admitted to her that he is a frequent user of marijuana, and her 17-year-old daughter is the subject of much school gossip about her alleged promiscuity. Her mother, who suffers from breast cancer, has recently moved in with her.

She has always been considered by her colleagues to be an exemplary teacher. Her students always do very well on standardized tests in reading and do an excellent job in producing classroom magazines and newspapers. Marilyn enjoys developing units that integrate language arts, the arts, and social studies; the units involve a great deal of student creative work. Occasionally one of her colleagues, Walter Michaelson, complains about too much student noise, but Principal Georgio has previously attributed the complaints to professional jealousy.

Her students' math scores have been only slightly above average; she admits that she does not like math very much but believes that she gives it the attention it deserves. She seems to spend a great deal of time in having the students work on math problems that are similar to those in the standardized test. Occasionally parents have expressed a concern to Marilyn that their children do not like mathematics. Marilyn minimized the concern, noting that elementary students "just don't like math."

Her colleagues consider her an informal leader. She has shared her yearly plans and her units with them. She provided informal leadership when her team moved to a whole language approach. She is usually assigned a student teacher, who all report that they enjoy working with her.

Since school opened in September, Georgio has been aware of a few minor concerns about her teaching. The fourth-grade teachers have complained that the third-grade team is not doing a good job of preparing students for fourth-grade mathematics. Marilyn seems to have taken the criticism personally, losing control of her temper in a September faculty meeting called to address the problem of declining math scores. During the month of October, Marilyn was absent for 3 days, reporting stress-produced illness. In his informal observations this year, Georgio has noted that many of the students, who were supposed to be involved in small-group work, often seemed to be off-task. Marilyn seemed oblivious to the problem, usually working with an individual student.

Principal Georgio is puzzled. He is inclined to ignore the issue in that he has two teachers who seem to need a great deal of help. On the other hand, he has a nagging sense that he should do something.

* * *

The challenge for principals in working with productive teachers is to recognize, reward, and support such teachers. Good teachers often complain that principals spend most of their time working with marginal teachers and novices. This chapter has several goals: (a) to clarify the nature of productive teaching, (b) to identify what all productive teachers need, (c) to explain how to make teacher leadership programs more effective, and (d) to suggest some ways of dealing with declining productivity.

Understanding the
Nature of Productive Teaching

As explained in Chapter 1, productive teachers are those who are competent and continue to grow, are able to reason abstractly and conceptually, are working at either an intermediate or advanced level of teaching, and are highly motivated with respect to their roles as teachers. Studies of expert teachers also cast some light on the characteristics of productive teachers (for review, see Berliner, 1986; Griffey & Housner, 1985; Jacullo-Noto, 1987; Kowalski & Weaver, 1987; Ropo, 1987). They work from a deeper knowledge base with respect to the curriculum, their students, and the science of teaching. Their educational goals are ambitious ones: they distinguish between short-term and long-term goals, they differentiate goals with respect to students, they want students to understand the conceptual nature of the subject, and they seek to develop problem-solving and critical-thinking skills.

Their planning is also complex and multifaceted. As they reflect about units and lessons, they envision alternative scenarios as to how the lesson might develop. They make effective long-term and unit plans that reshape the curriculum in subtle ways. And they make extensive provisions for assessing student learning.

As might be expected, their teaching evidences complexity and diversity. They use numerous routines to simplify classroom life and save time for learning. Within an instructional period they tend to move control from themselves to their students. They vary the instructional methodology as they receive formative assessment data about student learning. And they provide extensive scaffolding for student learning—repeating, giving examples, giving additional cues, and providing alternative ways of conceptualizing subject-based problems.

Supporting All Productive Teachers

All productive teachers need the active support of and recognition by their principal. However, the principal needs to provide these elements without seeming to play favorites or encouraging unproductive competition. Teachers tend to be egalitarian in their orientation: "We're all good teachers." And many "career ladder" programs have failed because they are antithetical to this core value of teachers. For example, in assessing the effects of 3 years of the Texas career ladder program, teachers identified these negative effects: it caused low morale, caused competition between teachers, was applied unfairly, and caused competition between teachers and administrators (Freiberg & Knight, 1991). And Devaney's (1987) research concluded that most teachers do not want upward movement in the organization.

Given these caveats, there is much that the principal can do to support all productive teachers.

Give Productive Teachers a Choice. The hope is that most productive teachers would want to work in the cooperative mode, in that they can exert such a powerful and positive influence. However, for reasons of their own, these teachers may wish to work in the self-directed mode. And, if district policies permit it, productive teachers should be able to function effectively without any formal supervision.

Encourage Cooperative Development. Although they should be given an option about their development, the principal should strongly encourage productive teachers to provide leadership in cooperative development programs. Although these programs need to be locally designed, certain guidelines can be drawn from the research. First, they will flourish only when the culture supports collegiality and cooperation. Second, they should be designed by the teachers with significant principal involvement. Next, they will probably function best if they are based on and use instructional teams, rather than becoming one more committee requiring teacher time. Small teams of three to six probably are more efficient than larger ones. And the cooperative program will be effective only if it has strong and active principal support.

BOX 4.1

Student Feedback Form

Directions. Read each statement below about our class. Indicate to what extent you agree or disagree with each statement by circling one of these letters: SA (*strongly agree*), A (*agree*), D (*disagree*), or SD (*strongly disagree*). Your teacher wants to know how you see these matters.

OUR CLASS . . .

1. Works together and cooperates in solving problems.	SA	A	D	SD
2. Finds this subject interesting.	SA	A	D	SD
3. Does the work assigned without causing trouble.	SA	A	D	SD
4. Learns what we are expected to learn.	SA	A	D	SD
5. Is graded fairly.	SA	A	D	SD
6. Understands what we are being taught.	SA	A	D	SD
7. Enjoys coming to this class.	SA	A	D	SD
8. Is challenged to do our best.	SA	A	D	SD
9. Can get the help we need when we need it.	SA	A	D	SD
10. Understands the importance of what we are learning.	SA	A	D	SD

AND ONE GENERAL QUESTION:
What could the teacher do that would help you learn more?

As explained in Chapter 3, the work done by collegial teams can take several forms: (a) action research that addresses major school and classroom problems, (b) professional dialogues based on current reading, (c) curriculum development that takes the form of units and learning materials that can be shared, and (d) peer observation and peer coaching for specific skill development.

Suspend Formal Evaluation. Formal evaluations tend to be a waste of time for productive teachers and for the principal as well. If productive teachers are actively involved in staff development and are included in the principal's informal observation plan, then there is no need for formal evaluation, at least until there are signs of declining productivity.

Provide Alternative Approaches for Feedback About Performance. Even though they need not be involved in formal supervisory processes,

BOX 4.2

Discussion Guide

Directions. The following guidelines, drawn from the research and the experience of effective teachers, provide some direction for analyzing class discussions and making them more effective.

Discussions will usually be more effective if teachers . . .

1. Ensure that students have a good knowledge base, checking throughout on the soundness of student knowledge.
2. When appropriate, arrange classroom seating so that students face each other and are no further than 10 feet apart from those they face.
3. Provide specific objectives for the discussion.
4. Ask open-ended questions that facilitate student thinking.
5. Respond appropriately to student answers.
6. Encourage students to speak directly to each other, rather than addressing all communication through the teacher.
7. Solicit student answers so that all students contribute to the discussion.
8. Use student answers to advance the discussion.
9. Encourage students to summarize and synthesize.
10. Enable students to evaluate the discussion.

they still can profit from constructive feedback about their performance. If they are working with colleagues in a cooperative mode, then the feedback can come from colleagues. If they are teaching with colleagues in a team teaching program, then feedback can come from the teaching team.

Feedback from students can be reinforcing and encouraging; it can also help productive teachers identify areas they wish to develop. If student feedback is to be used, the following conditions should prevail: (a) the feedback should not be used as part of the formal evaluation process, (b) the feedback should not have to be shared with anyone, and (c) as far as possible, the feedback should be descriptive, not evaluative. To accomplish this last condition, productive teachers may wish to use a form similar to the one shown in Box 4.1. Observe that it emphasizes "our class," not "our teacher."

Productive teachers can also get feedback by analyzing videotapes of their own teaching. However, they will gain the greatest benefit if they have some guidance about how to analyze their tapes. That guidance can come from a peer or from materials the principal provides. For example, a form similar to the one shown in Box 4.2 can be used by the teacher interested in improving discussion skills.

Give Productive Teachers Praise. Praise is a powerful motivator when it is timely, specific, and merited. General praise not focused on a specific performance is often viewed as insincere. In too many instances, the only praise that productive teachers receive is during an end-of-year evaluation conference. The best way for the principal to give the right kind of praise is by making positive comments after an informal observation. Contrast the following two comments:

GENERAL (offered after 6 months of never having observed teaching): You're doing a wonderful job this year.

SPECIFIC AND TIMELY (offered the day after making an informal observation): I really appreciated the way you were using peer teaching to clarify those complex concepts.

Keep Productive Teachers Informed. Productive teachers want to stay up to date, and they respect a principal who is on top of current educational issues. A principal who engages in professional dialogue with productive teachers conveys positive messages to them about the principal's professionalism. Secondary teachers especially need to believe that the principal has a general knowledge of new developments in their field.

Provide Productive Teachers With Quality Resources. Productive teachers especially will need ready access to high-quality professional resources that keep them current in the field, make them aware of developing trends, and assist them in fostering their own professional growth. Each school should have its own library of books, journals, video- and audiotapes, and software programs. Each of the major professional associations, including the National Association of Secondary School Principals (NASSP), publishes such materials. Productive teachers also need fiscal resources that enable them to participate in conferences and workshops. The leadership training provided by NASSP is known to be of excellent quality and would be highly useful to productive teachers interested in playing a leadership role. Three of the NASSP programs should be of special interest here: *Leader 1 2 3; Leadership Early Assessment Program;* and *Changing Times, Changing Schools, Changing Leadership.*

Providing Special
Leadership Opportunities

Productive teachers who are interested in serving as teacher-leaders can give a great deal to the school and also foster their professional development by carrying out several types of leadership roles. Some productive teachers want only the opportunity to teach and are reluctant to take on additional burdens of leadership. Therefore, teacher leadership should be seen as an opportunity for those wishing it, not as a requirement for all.

This leadership can take the form of the following:

1. Playing an active role on the school-based management or school improvement team
2. Mentoring novice teachers
3. Serving as an adjunct faculty member in a university teacher education program
4. Developing new curricula
5. Producing instructional materials
6. Organizing and leading staff development programs
7. Leading cooperative teams in their professional development
8. Serving as a grade-level or departmental leader
9. Planning and implementing special projects to involve parents
10. Serving as a content consultant or specialist
11. Carrying out systematic and classroom-based research

In that this expanded concept of teacher leadership is a relatively new phenomenon, its research base is somewhat limited. However, a review of that research and the authors' experience both suggest some guidelines for making such programs more effective (see Fay, 1992; Fullan, 1994; Lieberman, 1992; Miller, 1992; Wasley, 1991).

Be Sure the Antecedent Conditions Are Present

The antecedent conditions are those factors that must be present before the teacher-leader program is implemented. Four conditions are important. The first is a culture that values teacher leadership. If the administration and faculty do not truly value it but adopt it as one more educational fad, then it will not flourish. The second condition is a vision of school improvement that embodies teacher leadership as one of its vital elements. Thus, teacher leadership is related to a more comprehensive program of school improvement: It has a focus and a purpose. Third, from the outset there is significant teacher involvement at both an individual and organizational level. Individual teachers should work together with the principal to design the program so that it reflects their needs and goals. Teacher leadership programs imposed by the principal almost always have failed. The teachers' union or professional organization also should have input into the design process to ensure that the program honors the teacher contract. Finally, there needs to be strong principal leadership. Teacher leadership should never become an attempt to compensate for weak principal leadership. Here is the paradox: The more effective the principal, the more effective is teacher leadership.

Build Quality Foundations for the Program

The quality foundations are the major process and content components of the program. Several elements need to be present if the program is to succeed, according to the research in the field.

Role Clarity Emphasizing the Classroom. The program should specify very clearly the specific roles that teacher leaders are to play. Those roles should be closely related to the classroom. Teacher-leader programs that involve teachers as quasi-administrators represent a waste of talent.

Effective Structures With Legitimate Power. The work performed by teacher leaders should take place within such formal structures as the school improvement team, a curriculum task force, or a peer coaching program. The formal structure provides some stability and also becomes a means of legitimizing the role. Teacher leaders need a power base, and part of that power base needs to come from a formal organizational structure.

Desirable Incentives for Both Leaders and Colleagues. As Wasley (1991) points out, incentives for participating in the teacher-leader program should be made available to both the teacher leaders and the rest of the faculty. Those involved as leaders need incentives to compensate for their special efforts. The rest of the faculty need to believe that the program has some payoff for them. Such rewards need not be monetary ones. Several studies indicate that teachers are more motivated by such intrinsic rewards as seeing evidence of student growth than they are by so-called merit pay programs (see, e.g., McLaughlin & Yee, 1988).

Effective Training That Provides Access to Knowledge. New leadership roles require new skills and current knowledge. Some of that training will focus on skills required for any leadership program. Fullan (1994) identifies four knowledge areas that should be included in any leadership training program: (a) knowledge of teaching and learning, (b) knowledge of collegiality, (c) knowledge of educational contexts (parents, schools, communities, business, social agencies), and (d) knowledge of the change process. He also emphasizes the importance of continued growth for teacher leaders and a sense of moral purpose. In addition to such common elements, the training program should also develop role-specific skills. For example, a teacher curriculum-leader should understand the methods for developing integrated curriculum units that reflect a constructivist perspective.

Quality Time to Enable Leaders to Succeed. All reports of teacher leadership programs underscore the critical need for teacher leaders to have time for the jobs they have been assigned. They should not be punished for serving as leaders by having to surrender their own time to do the job. Providing released time for teacher leaders will obviously require the allocation of scarce fiscal resources. If the program is successful, the investment will have great payoff.

Evaluation Processes That Identify Problems and Assess Effectiveness. The best programs will include formative assessment processes for identifying emerging problems. Several problems can be anticipated, based on reports by teacher leaders: feelings of loneliness, as the role reduces their informal relationships with peers; role overload, as they try to do an excellent job in the classroom while struggling with the demands of a leadership role; and stress caused by the tension between collegiality and authority, as they work with colleagues who may be reluctant to accept their leadership. The principal should monitor the program by observing leaders at work, by conferring with leaders and other teachers from time to time, and by assessing the quality of products. Through formative monitoring, the principal can identify emerging problems and work with the teacher leaders to solve them.

The program should also provide for summative assessments at the end of the school year. Here more formal measures can be used: Surveys of teachers and structured interviews with teacher leaders would probably be most useful.

Teacher leadership holds great promise for both the school and the productive teachers involved. However, poorly designed and badly implemented programs are too costly to countenance.

Responding to Declining Productivity

As explained in Chapter 1, there seem to be two critical junctures in the stages of teachers' development in relationship to their productivity. Teachers with 7 to 18 years of experience either see the time as one of experimentation and activism, in which they remain productive, or as one of self-doubt and reassessment, when disenchantment with the profession and the schools sets in and their productivity diminishes. The next period, from 19 to 30 years of experience, also is a time of divergence. For many, it is a time of self-acceptance and serenity, when their productivity manifests itself in a self-confident approach to their students and the subject. For others, it becomes a time of conservatism, when their complaints and criticisms reduce their productivity.

Although a knowledge of the stages of teacher development should be of some assistance in recognizing the signs of declining productivity, it makes more sense for the principal to be conscious of individual behavior that suggests diminishing productivity may be occurring. In presenting these signs, it should be emphasized, of course, that even the best teachers have an "off" year once in a while. Teaching is so demanding that it is extremely difficult for anyone to maintain a high level of productivity year after year.

However, there are some general signs that principals should investigate if they appear with some consistency:

- Increased absence from school
- Withdrawal from leadership roles and sponsorship of extracurricular activities
- Increasing negativism about students and their parents
- The use of old lesson plans and learning materials
- More frequent use of seat work as a learning activity
- Declining interest in staff development activities
- Increasing isolation, as shown in resistance to collegial programs

These behaviors may suggest that the teacher is moving from productivity to passivity. The need is for a sensitive principal to recognize the signs and to explore them with the teacher, without pretending to be a psychologist or spiritual adviser.

The exploration can perhaps best take place in an open discussion with the teacher that raises the issue without being accusatory or confrontational. This is a very difficult conference to hold, because it may be the first time in several years that the teacher has received any negative feedback. The principal's goals are several: (a) to make the teacher aware of the principal's concerns, (b) to give the teacher ample opportunity to present the teacher's perspective, and (c) to engage with the teacher in cooperative problem solving that keeps the focus on student learning.

The following is how such a conference might begin:

Sue, I wanted a chance to talk with you about your teaching, as you perceive it. I should emphasize that this is not an evaluation conference, and I do not consider your teaching unsatisfactory. But I do have some concerns. However, I would rather begin by understanding your perspective. As you compare your work this year with what you accomplished last year, what are the major differences you see?

If the teacher responds by agreeing that there has been some decline in productivity, then they can both move into a problem-solving mode. If the teacher responds with defensiveness and denial, the principal should note just a few indicators of the decline, without overwhelming the teacher with too much negative feedback. The teacher should then have an opportunity to explain his or her perceptions of the issue. If the teacher insists that there is no problem, then the conference should end with both agreeing that there is a need for additional data.

The interventions used to halt declining productivity will obviously be affected by the nature of the problem. However, the authors' experience suggests that several of the following strategies might be generally effective:

- Assign the teacher a special responsibility, one that the teacher can carry out effectively
- Provide the resources for the teacher to attend professional conferences or special workshops
- Arrange for the teacher to have released time, as long as such arrangements do not impact negatively on other teachers
- Give the teacher a new teaching assignment, either in the same school or in a different school, if that seems desirable

Principals should keep in mind, however, that all teachers have their off years and should not overreact if the slump seems only temporary.

Inducting Novice Teachers

Portrait of Morgan Humphrey

Morgan Humphrey is a new member of the Central Middle School's eighth-grade team, teaching math and science. He was discharged from the army 2 years ago and was certified in a special 1-year program for adults wishing to make a career change. Before entering the military, he had completed a bachelor of science degree, with a major in biology, at the state university. He is 40 years old, unmarried, and seems to be something of a loner. Principal Watson selected him, after some initial doubts, because Watson believed that she needed a strong disciplinarian for low-ability eighth graders.

To aid in the induction process, Watson had asked Joanne Washington, an African American woman, to serve as his mentor; she is considered to be one of the best teachers in the school. Watson's charge to Washington was a simple and direct one: "Help him become part of the team, and give him whatever help he needs to get over the rough spots."

However, there have been some early signs of trouble. In conferring with Humphrey just two weeks ago, Humphrey complained about "bossy women," making specific references to the fact that he differed with Washington in her approach to student discipline: "Like a lot of women, she's too soft on those kids, especially the minority kids from the housing project; they need a firm hand."

In a follow-up conference between Washington and Watson, Washington admitted to some real problems. "He doesn't want to work with his team. He rarely takes an active part in team meetings. He complains that we're all too soft on students. I have made one classroom observation. He had good order, but the students spent most of their time working on drill sheets. Every time I made a suggestion in the conference, he would smile and say, 'You're right, Miss Washington.' "

Watson is similarly troubled by her relationship with Humphrey. He seems at times to be slightly condescending to her. Every time she makes a suggestion, he smiles and says, "Yes, boss."

Watson has made two formal observations of Humphrey's teaching. In both instances, she found the classroom climate to be one of teacher-student formality, student passivity, and strict compliance with posted rules. Humphrey made it clear that he was in charge; he had a baseball bat hanging from the wall, with a sign saying "The Persuader." The first lesson emphasized only the memorization of scientific terminology. Humphrey had a large chart of an amoeba on the classroom wall, with all its parts numbered and labeled, even though the eighth-grade science curriculum emphasized earth and space science. In the second lesson, students spent most of classroom time working on computational problems in mathematics, while Humphrey checked their work individually. In the first postobservation conference, Humphrey explained that he felt the students needed a solid foundation in the biological sciences before they could understand earth science. When Watson suggested some hands-on science work, Humphrey readily agreed, explaining that he had planned for such work after the students had learned the key concepts. When Watson suggested in the second conference that Humphrey give greater attention to problem solving in mathematics, Humphrey again agreed, explaining that he planned to teach problem solving after students had learned "the basics."

Watson is not sure what she should do about Humphrey. It is evident that the mentoring relationship is not working out. Humphrey has good discipline but is insensitive to student's needs.

* * *

Principals should give special attention to the development of novice teachers. Reliable estimates indicate that approximately 30% of beginning teachers will leave the profession during their first 2 years, a figure that represents a considerable waste of resources (Schlechty & Vance, 1983). And all the evidence suggests that most of these novice teachers will experience serious problems in teaching students. The discussion that follows reviews what is known about the characteristics and problems of beginning teachers. The rest of the chapter explains how to meet the special needs of novices.

Understanding the Characteristics and Problems of Novices

Although novice teachers differ considerably in their individual traits, a growing body of knowledge can provide some useful generalizations for principals and mentors who work with them (for review, see Berliner, 1986; Dunn, Taylor, Gillig, & Henning, 1987; Griffey and Housner, 1985; Jacullo-Noto, 1987; Ropo, 1987). Box 5.1 summarizes this research, and the major elements are discussed following.

Novices tend to have a limited knowledge base (about the subject, about students, and about pedagogical procedures) and function chiefly at a concrete cognitive level. They have very general goals, and are often chiefly concerned with students' personalities. Their planning tends to be inflexible, short-term, and management focused, making few provisions for assessment. In their teaching, they want to control all learning, have a limited number of classroom routines for repetitive activities (such as collecting homework), and rely chiefly on a direct instruction model.

Because of these limitations, they encounter somewhat predictable problems in the classroom. Several studies of the problems reported by novice teachers indicate that the following difficulties are most frequently encountered (listed in rank order of frequency; see Veenman, 1984):

1. Handling classroom discipline

BOX 5.1

Characteristics of a Novice Teacher

Knowledge

1. Tends to think at concrete level
2. Categorizes problems at a rather low theoretical level
3. Has limited metacognitive abilities in planning and monitoring
4. Has superficial knowledge of subject
5. Has limited number of knowledge schemata
6. Has limited knowledge of nature of students; concerned about backgrounds of individual students
7. Has limited procedural knowledge

Educational Goals

1. Is concerned with socialization of students and development of their personalities
2. Tends not to differentiate goals in relation to students' developmental levels
3. Sets rather general subject area goals
4. Sets few long-term goals

Planning

1. Shows little flexibility in planning
2. Is seemingly unaware of individual differences
3. Seems insensitive to the deep structure of the environment and how it will affect planning
4. Is concerned primarily with lesson management
5. Makes few provisions for student evaluation
6. Doesn't differentiate in relation to classes
7. Often forgets to plan for special materials and equipment
8. Does very little long-term planning or curriculum redesigning

Teaching

1. Has limited repertoire of routines—routines are less efficient and their use is often unpredictable
2. Tends to retain control of all learning
3. Makes lengthy presentations—does not vary presentation method
4. Uses longer and more frequent transitions
5. Seems to be insensitive to and unaware of individual problems—concerned only with class as a whole
6. Is more subject to manipulation by students
7. Does little assessment of student learning
8. Provides very little scaffolding; relies upon repetition
9. Uses fewer activity structures
10. Tends not to make effective use of student answers
11. Tends not to regroup for instruction

2. Motivating students
3. Dealing with individual differences
4. Assessing students' work
5. Maintaining effective relations with parents
6. Organizing class work

Principals should keep in mind, however, that these generalizations do not apply to all novice teachers. The authors' experience suggests, in fact, that novices can probably be divided into three groups. There are, first of all, "the naturals," a small number of novices who function as experienced teachers. Because they have had excellent preparation programs and possess the personal traits that make it easy for students to like them, they do not encounter major problems. Second, there are "the losers," a small number of novices whose failures are deeply ingrained. They are weak teachers who will continue to have major problems even after a few years' experience.

By far the largest number of novice teachers are those who are "the struggling beginners," whose problems are developmental ones. Their problems surface primarily because of lack of experience. Even the best student teaching programs cannot fully prepare novices for the realities of planning for and teaching their own classes on a full-time schedule. Unlike the marginal teachers discussed in the next chapter, they are not failing as teachers. Instead, they are experiencing growing pains, the stresses that come from having to master a very complex set of skills under quite difficult conditions.

This analysis of the novice teacher suggests that most novice teachers will have the following needs: a teachable assignment, supportive peer groups, intensive evaluation, and intensive development. These elements are discussed in the sections that follow.

Providing a Teachable Assignment

Typically the novice teacher, especially in the secondary school, "floats" from room to room, is given multiple teaching assignments, and is assigned the most difficult students. This traditional approach to teacher assignment simply reflects the weight given in the organization to the power that derives from seniority and is not a reflection of principal insensitivity or ignorance. However, the need to give novices a teachable assignment is so great that principals are strongly encouraged to challenge the seniority system, making it clear to experienced teachers that ensuring the success of the school is more important than providing perquisites to those who have taught the longest.

The first step in providing a teachable assignment is to assign the novice to a grade-level or subject-matter team, encouraging experienced team members to make the novice feel at home. As noted in Chapter 3, the novice should have an opportunity to work with team colleagues in a cooperative mode, as well as receiving intensive development from the principal or a mentor.

Next, the principal should attempt to provide a supportive physical environment, assigning permanent classroom space to the teacher. If permanent classroom space is not available, then the novice should be given office space for preparing lessons, conferring with colleagues, and working with individual students.

The next step is to build a supportive schedule. That means, first of all, ensuring that the novice has adequate preparation time. In addition to the standard preparation time given to all teachers, the novice ideally should be provided with one or two unscheduled periods each week, to be reserved for the special *orientation network* meetings explained below. If possible, all novice teachers in that building should have the same preparation period in common, to facilitate group orientation. Some schools have found it a very useful practice to give each novice four fifths of the standard teaching load, as a means of ensuring a successful first year.

It would also be important to assign to the novice teacher students who will not present an undue challenge to the teacher. The following kinds of classes, which pose special problems for all teachers, should be assigned to the most competent faculty: (a) extremely heterogeneous classes, (b) classes with many special-needs students, and (c) classes that include many students who have had a history of disruptive behavior. Also, novice teachers in secondary schools should not be given more than two preparations; novices find that planning and preparing for three or four different subjects or grade levels is an overwhelming demand.

Providing these special accommodations to the novice teacher may engender some resentment from the experienced faculty. Here the principal needs to provide leadership in convincing the veterans that so-called "babying" of the novice will in the long run pay great dividends to the school.

Providing Supportive Groups

The second need is for supportive groups. Two groups are suggested here. As noted above, the novice should be assigned to an instructional team, an active group of professionals who are working together for their development as a team and as individuals. The team should engage in its own version of cooperative development, fully involving the novice in all those activities. As the team works together, they should make a special effort to include the novice and to support the novice with timely praise and encouragement.

The second group is identified as the orientation network. This should be a group of novice teachers who meet periodically with the principal. As explained previously, time for these group sessions should be provided by scheduling all members with the same preparation periods once or twice each week. If there are not enough novices to constitute a group, the principal can collaborate with the principal of a school nearby to set up a combined group, include in the group a small number of other interested teachers, or meet individually with each novice teacher. The first few sessions should be devoted to an orientation to the community, the district, and the school. The agenda for succeeding sessions should be set by the members as they identify problems they are encountering or raise questions that need answers.

These groups will need effective leadership provided by an administrator or senior faculty member who understands group processes. Leaders will differ in the way they lead these groups. The groups will be most successful, however, if certain guidelines are observed. First, minimize lecture and maximize discussion. If information must be presented, present it in print form and then discuss its implications. Second, give the group meeting a problem-solving focus. For example, instead of lecturing about community resources, the leader would present the issue as a problem to be solved: "In what ways could you individually use community resources—and what cautions should you observe?" Finally, encourage open reflection, developing a climate in which participants feel free to try out ideas in a supportive environment.

Obviously, one of the primary functions of these groups is to provide continuing orientation, focusing on emerging issues of consequence to the group. Such an approach is much more effective than the "orientation day" typically held before school opens. In too many of these sessions, novices are overwhelmed with information they do not need at that time (such as how the transportation system operates). Their minds are on their rooms, their classes, their curriculum, and their materials; those are the pressing concerns that opening-of-school sessions should address.

Structuring Intensive Evaluation

As explained in Chapter 3, novices will require intensive evaluation by an administrator. Although this book is not centrally concerned with teacher evaluation, the close relationship of evaluation and supervision suggests the need for a general discussion. The processes used to evaluate new teachers are usually dictated by district policies, and each administrator will have his or her own approach to teacher evaluation. Therefore, the recommendations made below are offered as general guidelines, not as rigid prescriptions.

Principals should evaluate novice teachers to make an early determination as to whether a novice seems to be a natural, a loser, or a struggling beginner. The following process should enable principals to accomplish that goal.

1. Begin with a taking-stock conference that deals with the following issues: (a) state and district policies governing evaluation of nontenured teachers, (b) the criteria and the forms to be used, (c) the processes that will be employed, along with a tentative time line, (d) the evaluator's role, and (e) the relationship of evaluation and development. If there are several novices to be evaluated, they could all meet with the administrator in a group conference.

2. Make a few informal observations during the second and third week of school. As explained in Chapter 2, these drop-in

visits, lasting only 5 to 10 minutes, should be made to the classrooms of all teachers, as a means of reinforcing good teaching and keeping the principal visible. They also serve as a distant early warning system for detecting emerging problems. They are especially important for gaining some informal impressions of the novice's overall effectiveness. Because of their informal nature, they should be documented by completing a form similar to the one shown in Figure 2.2. Each teacher should receive a copy and be encouraged to discuss any of the questions noted. Note that the form identifies "questions" the observer had, not "problems" or "areas for improvement." Because the observations are very brief, the question form is more appropriate.

3. Give the novice a chance to get settled. Although it is important for the administrator to know very early if there are serious problems, the evaluation system will be more equitable if novices know that they have a 1- or 2-month grace period free of formal evaluation. This grace period will give them time to get to know their students, the curriculum, and their materials. If the informal observations suggest that the novice is experiencing major problems, then the formal evaluation process might begin earlier. One experienced principal also suggests that the principal should do some proactive work with the parents whose children are being taught by novices.

4. Make two classroom observations in October, followed by an evaluation conference. Some experts recommend that the principal also hold a preobservation conference, to review lesson plans. The difficulty here is that evaluation observations in general should be unannounced, to be sure that the teacher does not present a carefully rehearsed and atypical performance. If the observation is unannounced, then the preobservation conference would be counterproductive. Principals should resolve this issue by reviewing district policy and their own experience.

If possible, these two observations should be on consecutive days, of the same class, to give the evaluator a tentative sense of how one lesson is related to another. These observations should focus on the evaluative criteria, with evidence collected for each criterion. In general, experts recommend that evaluators use the following process in making such observations:

- Make a detailed transcript of all teaching-learning transactions, noting the time of each transaction.
- As the class ends, make a tentative holistic judgment of the overall effectiveness of that lesson.
- Use the transcript and the holistic assessment to complete the evaluation form.

After making these two successive observations, the evaluator should hold a debriefing conference to share the results of the evaluative observation. Unlike developmental conferences that are problem solving in orientation, the evaluation conference should be more direct in that the teacher's overriding concern is, "How did I do?" As an example, the evaluator might say very directly, "That lesson was satisfactory. Here is the evaluation form and the supporting notes. Please review them so we can talk in more detail about the reasons for the evaluation." The debriefing conference should end with the administrator and novice agreeing on a professional development plan, which provides specific information about what skills need to be developed and how and when they will be developed.

The professional development plan should be given to the mentor, if one has been assigned, who will be responsible for its implementation.

5. In late October or early November, hold a *support skills* conference. The support skills are three skills that are needed for effective instruction but ordinarily cannot be assessed through direct observation: (a) student assessment, (b) instructional planning, and (c) student record keeping. The teacher should be instructed to bring to the session the following materials: (a) a test that has been given and graded, (b) a test that will be given, (c) yearly plans, (d) one unit plan, (e) daily plans for that unit, and (f) the student record book. The evaluator should assess them critically, offer suggestions for improvement, and note areas of strength. All

these actions should be carefully documented in a form identified as *Professional Development Plan: Support Skills.*

This form should also be shared with the mentor, who will provide any follow-up needed.

6. In mid-November, hold a second taking-stock conference. In this conference, focus on answering these key questions: Is this novice probably a natural, a loser, or a struggling beginner? At this time, what is the prognosis for the novice's success? By analyzing all data, the evaluator should make one of three decisions:

   - The teacher is a natural, whose overall performance is clearly satisfactory. The teacher can be moved to the standard evaluation track and satisfy development requirements through cooperative work with the team.
   - The teacher is probably a struggling beginner. The intensity of the evaluation can be reduced, while support and development should continue at the same level.
   - The teacher is probably a loser. All data indicate clearly that the teacher's performance is unsatisfactory; emergency measures are needed.

This key decision should be made by putting the first 3 months in perspective. The following are the issues that should be examined in making this determination:

- Has there been evidence of gradual improvement? Lack of improvement suggests that the novice is a loser.
- Is the novice aware of any specific problems? Naturals and struggling beginners usually ask for help when they need it; losers often try to hide problems or deny their existence.
- Has the novice been open to constructive feedback? Struggling beginners usually welcome assistance; losers get defensive.
- Is the novice's performance uneven—satisfactory in some dimensions, unsatisfactory in others? Losers tend to be unsatisfactory across all dimensions.

If the problems seem deeply ingrained and are not solely developmental ones, then the evaluator, the mentor, and the teacher should together design an intervention program that will enable the novice to make significant improvement. Those interventions might include changing the teaching assignment, getting assistance from district supervisors, increasing the coaching, hiring a substitute to give the novice a chance to regroup, or having the novice do a guided observation of a skilled teacher. All these actions should be carefully documented in case a decision is made to terminate the contract.

The evaluation system recommended above is intended to be fair, rigorous, and professionally sound. Its importance cannot be overstated: Experts are in general agreement that too many incompetent teachers sneak through the gates because principals are too soft and excessively idealistic in their approach to teacher evaluation.

Providing Intensive Development

The most vital part of the entire program for novice teachers is intensive development. This intensive development is ordinarily provided by a mentor, a highly skilled and experienced teacher. However, the principal, assistant principal, or district supervisor may serve as mentor if that seems desirable. The following discussion examines the general issue of mentoring and then recommends a process of intensive development.

The Mentoring Process

Regardless of who performs the role, four processes are crucial for success: (a) clarify the role, (b) select and assign the mentors, (c) train for mentoring, and (d) provide support.

Clarify the Role. Many mentoring programs have failed because of the ambiguous nature of the role. Therefore, the first step is to clarify the role's general orientation and its specific responsibilities. Administrators should make clear that the general orientation of the role is development, not evaluation. Many mentoring programs have encountered difficulty because the mentor was expected to be both a source of support and a contributor to the evaluation process. A clear distinction is strongly recommended here: Mentors should support and coach; administrators should evaluate. No data developed in the mentoring relationship should be shared with evaluators, except at the novice's request.

The principal should clearly delineate the specific responsibilities of the role. Ordinarily the mentor will carry out several functions— orienting the novice to the team and the school, clarifying informal norms of the organization, explaining district policies that impinge on the novice, providing access to resources, assisting with instructional planning, observing and giving feedback, coaching, and providing empathic support when needed.

Select and Assign the Mentors. If peer mentors are used, two options are available for assigning and selecting them. When a strong team structure is in place, some administrators find it most effective to request each team to identify one of its members who will serve as mentor for all novice teachers. Others establish a pool of qualified teachers and then attempt to match mentor and novice.

Regardless of the option chosen, all mentors should be carefully selected based on the criteria that the mentor is strongly motivated to mentor, understands the special needs of beginners, has mastered at least the intermediate skills of teaching, knows how to coach, communicates effectively, can provide empathic support, has high credibility with the rest of the faculty, and has an in-depth knowledge of the community and the school.

If a pool of qualified mentors has been established, then the principal should attempt to match the mentor and the novice. According to the research, the important matching characteristics are that the mentor (a) has an educational ideology compatible with that of the novice assigned, (b) has a teaching assignment similar to the novice's, (c) is readily accessible, with a classroom near the novice's, and (d) is of the same gender as the novice. This last matching factor perhaps needs special note here. One expert (Galvez-Hjornevik, 1986) points out that female-male combinations encounter special problems: Female novices who work with male mentors report they often experience overprotectiveness, greater social distance, and general discomfort. In addition, male and female partners must deal with the sexual tensions that may develop and the public scrutiny that follows.

Train the Mentors. All mentors will need special training in the skills of mentoring. The following skills should be developed:

- Understanding and clarifying the mentor-novice relationship
- Orienting novices
- Providing empathic support
- Diagnosing novices' needs and strengths
- Collecting and analyzing diagnostic and focused observational data
- Providing developmental feedback
- Coaching for skill development
- Helping novices solve classroom problems
- Working collaboratively with novices to solve problems in their relationship

Provide Support. Finally, all mentors will need ongoing support. The most important support is the time needed to do the job: The major complaints of mentors is the lack of quality time. If possible, therefore, the mentor should be given released time to accomplish the several functions. The second resource is materials needed to do the job—professional training tapes, camcorders for taping lessons, monitors for viewing tapes, and professional books.

Also, mentors will need the interpersonal support of the principal, who should give the mentor timely praise and stress to the faculty the importance of the mentoring role.

Intensive Development

As explained previously, *intensive development* is the term used here to identify a special use of clinical supervision. Its main purpose is to help the novice develop and refine teaching skills. In implementing intensive development, the mentor should use a step-by-step approach that does not overwhelm the novice with too many recommendations for immediate implementation. The following discussion explains one such approach that has been used successfully. Note, however, that the mentor should use these strategies flexibly. If it appears that the novice is making excellent progress, then the mentor can reduce the frequency and intensity of the developmental approach.

Hold a Taking-Stock Conference. This initial taking-stock conference should deal with the personal and professional background of each, the nature of the relationship, the novice's and the mentor's belief systems, the novice's perceptions of strengths and weaknesses, and the overall plan for the development of the novice. The goal is to establish a solid foundation for the professional relationship.

Make the First Diagnostic Observation. As explained in Chapter 3, a diagnostic observation is one in which the observer scans all teacher and student behaviors, in an attempt to identify significant strengths and weaknesses. The first diagnostic observation should be an announced one to give the novice an opportunity to make special plans and preparations.

Here the preobservation conference would be most useful; it would provide the teacher with an opportunity to discuss the class, review the plans, and get the mentor's input.

In making this diagnostic observation, the mentor should note all significant teacher and student behaviors and the time they occurred. A sample form is shown in Box 5.2.

The goal is to make a detailed and comprehensive record—one that will enable the mentor to diagnose strengths and weaknesses and that can be shared with the novice. Whenever feasible, the mentor should note in the "student behavior" column specific data about the number involved in a particular behavior. In that the observational record will be accessible to the novice, it should not include the mentor's evaluations of what occurred.

Analyze the Observational Data. Shortly after the class has concluded and while the classroom transactions are still fresh in memory, the mentor should analyze the observational record independently.

BOX 5.2

Diagnostic Observation Form

Time	Teacher Behaviors	Student Behaviors
9:05	Sue at desk, checking homework papers.	Most students talking;
9:08	"Let's get to work now—you've had time	3 are out of seats.
	to gossip."	About half continue to talk.

The focus of the analysis is to determine to what extent the novice has mastered the basic skills of teaching. If the district has identified such basic skills for purposes of evaluation and supervision, then the district formulation should be used to ensure that the developmental activities are congruent with the evaluation process.

One useful means of analyzing the observational data is to review the record, indicating in the margin whether a particular skill was being used effectively. For example, next to the entry shown in Box 5.2, the mentor might enter this code, –CC. This would indicate a potential weakness (shown by the minus sign) in classroom climate (indicated with the abbreviation CC).

This detailed analysis should enable the mentor to identify one or two strengths and one or two areas for improvement.

Conduct a Debriefing Conference. The observation and analysis should be accompanied by a debriefing conference whose purpose is to identify collaboratively the strengths and potential weaknesses of the novice. The mentor has a choice of two styles: direct and indirect. In the direct style, the mentor gives the observational notes with the coding to the novice with a general assessment: "The data suggest that you are very sound in content knowledge; you may need some help with classroom management." In the indirect approach, the mentor gives the novice an uncoded copy of the observational data and asks the novice, "As you reflect about this lesson and consider my observational notes, what strengths and areas for improvement do you note?"

For most novices the indirect approach would be more effective because it actively involves the teacher in shaping the developmental agenda. However, if the novice seems to lack the necessary insight, then a direct approach would be more appropriate. With either approach, the mentor should use a data-based problem-solving strategy, helping the novice make sense of the observational data and reflecting about his or her decision-making processes.

The conference should end with the mentor and the novice agreeing about the developmental agenda by identifying one skill that needs to be strengthened or refined.

Coach for Skill Development

Once that skill has been identified, then the mentor should coach the novice to acquire that skill. Most supervisors omit this crucial step, moving from observation to conference to observation again, without any coaching for skill acquisition.

The intensity of the coaching will vary with the novice's need and the mentor's time. The mentor should use the following coaching sequence selectively and flexibly.

1. Provide a knowledge base for the skill. The research is clear about the importance of developing a knowledge base for a skill teachers are attempting to master. If, for example, the novice needs to improve skill in leading a discussion, he or she should have knowledge about the following issues: (a) arranging seating for good discussion, (b) posing effective discussion issues, (c) asking stimulating questions, (d) listening and responding to student answers, (e) securing maximum involvement of all students, and (f) evaluating discussions. The knowledge base can be provided through books, videotapes, journal articles, and special materials. Glatthorn's (1990) book includes "coaching protocols" for 10 basic teaching skills; the coaching protocols provide the knowledge base needed to understand the importance of the skill and the knowledge that undergirds the skill. The mentor should provide the knowledge before the coaching session takes place.

2. When the actual coaching session begins, explain the skill in a step-by-step manner. Detailed explanations are necessary for skill mastery. In too many instances, supervisors make only

rather general suggestions: "You should get class started more efficiently." Contrast that with the following detailed explanation:

> Have a "sponge" activity on the board for students to do while class is assembling.
>
> Do a quick check of attendance by noting vacant seats.
>
> During the sponge activity, check their homework.
>
> Use a standard signal for getting student attention.
>
> Conduct a brief review of the previous day's learning.

3. Demonstrate the skill, step-by-step, in the coaching conference.
4. Provide opportunity for the novice to practice the skill in the coaching conference.
5. As soon as the practice is concluded, give the novice constructive feedback about the practice.
6. Arrange for the novice to use the skill independently, with feedback. Specific arrangements should be made for the novice to use the skill when the mentor can observe and give feedback.

Provide Focused Feedback

The mentor should then provide focused feedback about the use of the skill identified for development. Focused feedback comes from an observer who has agreed to focus on one aspect of teaching, such as asking questions. Diagnostic feedback is useful when teachers want to get a general picture of their teaching; focused feedback is better when teachers are trying to master one specific skill.

The most effective way to get focused feedback is to develop a focused feedback form that helps the observer get objective data. The focused feedback form lists the specific categories about which the novice wants information and presents them in a manner that will facilitate data collection and analysis. (One of the best sources for focused feedback forms is the book by Good & Brophy, 1991.)

Several methods are commonly used to get focused feedback. *Selected verbatim* is a running record of all the teacher's behaviors as they relate to a particular skill. For example, if the novice is focusing on responding to student answers, the mentor would note in chronological order all the responses the teacher made.

BOX 5.3

Checklist for Effective Explaining

Directions. For each behavior noted below, enter a tally for each time it is used.

1. Provides initial structure: connection with prior learning, reason for learning, verbal and visual overviews
2. Explains skills one step at a time
3. Provides verbal signals that help students understand the structure of the explanation
4. Uses strategies to facilitate concept attainment
5. Reviews important concepts
6. Reinforces verbal explanations with other approaches
7. Defines key concepts in terms students can understand
8. Helps students construct personal meaning by having them use their own representations
9. Monitors student attention and understanding, making needed corrections
10. Summarizes (or has students summarize) what was learned

Seating charts are used when the novice needs information about particular students. The novice prepares a seating chart with students' names, allowing sufficient space in each cell for observational coding. If, for example, the teacher was interested in increasing on-task student performance, he or she would ask the observer to note every time a particular student was off task.

Checklists are lists of specific behaviors that relate to a particular skill. Box 5.3 shows a checklist for the skill of "explaining effectively." The observer would note each time teachers used a behavior on the checklist.

Analytical charts take the form of matrices. Across the top are listed one set of conditions; down the left-hand side, the related responses or behaviors. The observer simply places a tally in each cell. Table 5.1 shows an analytical chart that could be used for analyzing how a teacher responds to student answers; the types of student answers are listed across the top, with the types of teacher responses down the left.

The focused observation, using the form, should be followed by a debriefing conference. The novice and the mentor together review the novice's achievement to that date. At this point they have three choices:

TABLE 5.1 Analytical Chart, Teacher Response

Teacher Response	Student Response					
	Mixed	Unclear	Correct	Wrong	Insightful	Irrelevant
Repeat		X				
Praise			X	X		
Probe	X					
Para-phrase		X				
Negate		X				
Use					X	

1. If the novice seems to need additional work on the first skill identified, continue to work on it as a means of ensuring mastery.
2. If the novice has mastered that skill but needs to work on a second skill, identify the next skill, either by planning another diagnostic observation or relying on the intuitive judgment of the novice and the mentor and proceed as before.
3. If the novice is making good progress and needs only continued support, reduce the intensity of the developmental process but maintain the support.

Again the emphasis is on a flexible approach that sees the relationship as an evolving one, depending on the novice's progress.

If the procedures above are implemented flexibly and effectively, only minor problems should develop. However, principals should be aware of and sensitive to the problems shown in Box 5.4 and take the necessary steps to prevent them.

Potential Problems
in the Novice Teacher Program

From the Novice's Perspective

1. Is not provided with a teachable assignment
2. Feels isolated and excluded from faculty groups
3. Is not evaluated closely and constructively
4. Is not provided with the help needed to improve
5. Has difficulty working with the mentor
6. Feels overwhelmed with observations, conferences, and coaching sessions
7. Believes that mentor and principal do not recognize the progress made; is caught in an inflexible program

From the Mentor's Perspective

1. Has not been trained sufficiently
2. Has not been given sufficient time
3. Experiences role conflict: is expected to develop and evaluate
4. Does not get sufficient input from the evaluation process
5. Has difficulty working with the novice

From the Principal's Perspective

1. Feels overwhelmed by the demands of the program
2. Attempts to standardize the program and as a result administers the program inflexibly
3. Does not communicate effectively with mentor
4. Does not give sufficient time and attention to evaluation
5. Resents being excluded from the development process and, as a result, assumes developmental responsibilities

6

Providing Help to Marginal Teachers

Portrait of Wilbert Martin

Wilbert Martin has been teaching high school English for 5 years now. He received tenure 2 years ago, recommended by a principal who has since retired. He is 27 years old, recently married, with one child; his wife is a science teacher in the district's middle school. Martin is slight of build, wears glasses, and acts in a deferential manner with all adults. His colleagues like him but do not seem to have much respect for him as a teacher.

The evidence now suggests that he should not have received tenure. Parents ask that their sons and daughters not be assigned to his classes. The most able students complain that they are not learning as much as they should, complaining to their guidance counselor that Martin spends all his time trying to discipline the class and asking them what they want to learn. Some of his students express a genuine affection for him: "He's an easy grader, and he makes English fun," is a typical comment.

Jasper Warren has been his principal for 2 years now. From the beginning he realized that Martin was having serious problems. Every time Warren made an informal observation, Martin would either have the students working in groups (usually in a slightly chaotic manner) or would be discussing with them what they wanted to study next.

The formal observations that Warren made each year yielded somewhat similar results. Warren would open the door to loud student noise, which would immediately diminish when students realized the principal was observing. The students would be sitting in small groups, in a climate of almost total disorder, usually arguing about topics that seemed to have no direct relationship with the district's curriculum. One unit seemed to be about dress styles and how they communicate; another was on the paranormal, with a strong emphasis on the legitimacy of parapsychology; a third was on sports heroes; the fourth, on rap music as poetry.

The postobservation conferences suggested that Martin does not believe he has a problem—or is not ready to admit that the problem exists. He defended the use of small groups by citing the research on cooperative learning and noting the recommendations of experts that the classroom should be a "social environment for learning." He defended his use of student input into the curriculum by arguing that it represented the best of "student-centered learning" and resulted in more student interest than that produced by the district guide, which he considered "irrelevant." However, in each case he agreed that he would exercise greater control over student discipline and give more attention to the district curriculum guide.

For 3 years now, the district has been requiring the administration of end-of-course tests. In the first 2 years, Martin's students scored at the bottom when compared with the rest of the teachers in the English department. The third year showed a slight improvement, but the scores still seem very low, given the abilities of the students. In faculty and departmental discussions of test results, Martin always attacks the tests as measuring inconsequential learning.

Helen Gurganus, the English department chair, has come to Warren for help. She believes that Martin is past the point of being helped and should be dismissed. Teachers assigned to rooms that adjoin his complain that the student noise in his classrooms disrupts their own attempts to teach. Martin seems to pay only lip service to the district curriculum guide, giving brief attention to district objectives only when he feels pressure. The units he devises seem increasingly bizarre.

Principal Warren is perplexed. Martin has received *satisfactory* ratings each year he has taught. Student attitudes seem mixed. Martin is able to cite research in defending how he teaches and what he teaches and seems to have a positive attitude toward supervision. But obviously there are major problems that need attention.

* * *

On every faculty, there are probably one or two teachers who can be classified as marginal. Unlike novices experiencing developmental problems, they are experienced teachers who, year after year, perform unsatisfactorily because of deeply ingrained problems. Because of the reluctance of principals to go through a complicated dismissal process, they continue to teach. One study concluded that, in a 2-year period, fewer than 0.6% of the teachers in California were dismissed for incompetence (Bridges, 1990). The costs of dismissing incompetent teachers seem staggering at times: One researcher documents a case study of teacher dismissal that cost the district $166,716 (Bridges, 1992).

In most cases, the poor quality of their performance is widely known—by school administrators, other teachers, the students, and the parents. They present a significant problem to themselves, to the schools where they teach, and to the profession. One expert in the field estimates that the number of students being taught by ineffective teachers exceeds the total combined enrollment of public school students in the fourteen smallest states (Bridges, 1990).

Understanding the Nature
of the Marginal Teacher

There has been relatively little research on marginal teachers because of the difficulty of identifying them for research purposes. The limited research available and the authors' experience suggest that they do share some common general traits and manifest some specific weaknesses.

Three general traits stand out. First, they are typically frustrated and do not find teaching satisfying. Even though they are reluctant to acknowledge their own problems, most know that things are not going well. Every day is a struggle to get through to students. Rather than examining their own deficiencies, they blame the students: Often they are the ones who complain most loudly in the faculty lounge about "kids and parents today." Bridges (1990) found that marginal teachers tend to deny a problem exists, blame the students and parents, or attack the administrator in response to administrative criticism.

Despite their lack of satisfaction, they are persistent, hanging on grimly to their jobs. They believe they lack satisfactory career alternatives: no jobs are available at their present salary level, they have too many years in the retirement system, or they do not want to spend the time and money to prepare themselves for other careers.

Finally, they are defensive. Their general reaction to feedback is either denial or superficial compliance. Some will argue about every suggestion offered. Others have mastered what they see as the game of supervision. They pretend to welcome criticism and deceptively promise to implement suggestions they consider unworkable. They see the principal's observations and conferences, coming only twice a year, as a small price to pay for job security.

These general traits are accompanied by some specific deficiencies. Bridges (1992) found that marginal teachers fail (a) to maintain discipline, (b) to treat students properly, (c) to impart subject matter effectively, (d) to accept teaching advice from superiors, (e) to demonstrate mastery of subject matter, and (f) to produce desired results.

Although marginal teachers share many of these characteristics, they also differ in some respects. Although it is usually unwise to classify teachers, certain tentative categories seem useful in understanding the phenomenon of marginality. The authors' experience suggests that the marginal performers can be classified into three types: "wimps," "martinets," and "buddies." Wimps are weak teachers who simply cannot manage classrooms. Students lack respect for them, showing their disrespect by acting disruptively and defying the teacher's attempts to establish order. Wimps spend most of their time by asking students to be quiet—to no avail. The wimp in fact spends much of the time pleading and bargaining with students—to be quiet, to do the assigned work, to stay on task.

Martinets are teachers who are obsessed with control. They control the grading process by setting impossible standards for most students. They almost seem to want a high failure rate as a badge of their toughness. They control student behavior by setting and enforcing rigid rules, using fear of punishment as a means of control. They control the curriculum by teaching the same highly structured content year after year. Typically they see themselves as subject matter experts who have little interest in students' concerns.

Buddies are chiefly middle school and high school teachers who want to be friends of students. They set low standards, especially for minority students, and give excessive praise and high grades for even poor performance. They anxiously ask students what they want to learn, believing that the curriculum should be totally student determined. Occasionally they try to become too close to students, asking inappropriate personal questions, spending too much time after school with them, and even getting too close physically.

Although the typology is useful for analyzing the problems marginal teachers face, principals should keep in mind the limitations of such systems. Teachers are individuals, and even those who share incompetence as a characteristic differ in many ways.

Regardless of the labels used and the individual differences encountered, the literature in the field and the authors' experience suggest that marginal teachers need a combination of rigorous evaluation and supportive development—the administrator's version of "tough love." Rigorous evaluation without supportive development is unfair to the teacher; supportive development without rigorous evaluation may turn out to be unfair to the school by keeping marginal teachers in the classroom.

Providing Intensive Evaluation

In designing and implementing an intensive evaluation program, the assumption is that in prior years the marginal teacher has received *satisfactory* ratings accompanied with specific recommendations for improvement—with no evidence that improvement has been made. The marginal teacher should now receive an intensive evaluation process that is both similar to and different from that provided to the novice teacher. The discussion that follows presents some general guidelines for evaluating marginal teachers; those desiring more detailed information may wish to consult the 1993 manual by Lawrence, Vachon, Leake, and Leake and Bridges's (1992) research-based report.

Ensure the Necessary Antecedent Conditions

Certain antecedent conditions should be in place, according to recent research (Bridges, 1992). First, there is a need for strong commitment from the top: The board and the superintendent need to commit themselves to strong support for the principal and the process. Second, the district should have a set of defensible criteria and an evaluation process that results in valid and consistent ratings. Third, the evaluators need to be trained, because the task is both a crucial and a complex one. One observer noted, for example, that it takes 6 years of training to become certified as a judge of cattle, but only 1 course to become an evaluator of teachers. Finally, adequate resources should be provided: Personnel and time are most crucial.

Select and Train the Evaluators

The first step is to decide who will conduct the evaluation and to ensure that the evaluators are trained. Although the principal should be primarily responsible for the evaluation, experts in the field recommend that two or three trained evaluators should be used in evaluations of marginal teachers (Beckham, 1981). Larger districts establish a pool of trained evaluators who assess performance full-time; some smaller districts contract with a consultant who is an expert in the field.

Develop a Schedule
for the Evaluation Process

In working with the marginal teacher, the principal is well advised to develop a specific schedule for all the observations, conferences,

---

BOX 6.1

Schedule for Evaluation of Marginal Teacher

Action	Date
1. Hold first taking-stock conference	9/2
2. Make first observation with conference	9/15
3. Share professional development plan with supervisor	9/16
4. Make second observation with conference	10/1
5. Hold support skills conference	10/15
6. Share support skills results with supervisor	10/16
7. Hold second taking-stock conference	11/3
8. Make third observation with conference	11/6
9. Make fourth observation with conference	12/5
10. Make fifth observation with conference	1/6
11. Hold third taking-stock conference	1/15
12. Make sixth observation with conference	2/15
13. Make seventh observation with conference	3/1
14. Hold fourth taking-stock conference	3/15
15. Initiate formal action to dismiss or recommend contract renewal	3/22

---

and administrative actions to ensure that a rigorous evaluation can take place while due process is provided the teacher. A sample schedule is shown in Box 6.1. Observe that it moves at an accelerated pace during the first semester and continues the evaluation process at a slightly slower pace during the first few months of the second semester. The timing of observations and conferences is planned so that formal action can be taken early, in late March or early April, giving the marginal teacher some time to explore his or her options.

It should be noted that some experts in the field recommend a greatly accelerated schedule. Lawrence et al. (1993) believe that the principal should conduct four formal observations in October, three in November, and three in December, with a summative evaluation in January. Although the more intensive evaluation will provide additional data, there are some problems here. The intensity of the process may become counterproductive, producing excessive stress in the teacher. The early determination of the unsatisfactory evaluation means that a weak teacher will function as a lame duck for an entire semester. Principals should resolve this important issue by reviewing district policy, assessing the number of marginal teachers, and reflecting about their own experience with marginal teachers.

In planning the schedule, the principal should be sure to sample all major parts of the teacher's assignment and vary the time of day and day of the week. One researcher observed that elementary teachers varied considerably in the way they taught mathematics and social studies (Stodolsky, 1984). Teachers also report variations in student responses depending on the time of the day and the day of the week: By the end of the school day the students and the teacher are both tired and by Friday afternoon, students have their minds on weekend activities.

Hold the Taking-Stock Conference

The principal begins the process by holding a taking-stock conference with the marginal teacher, one that is markedly different from the one held with the novice. The following represents the message the principal needs to convey during this conference:

> You have been placed on this intensive evaluation track because there are serious doubts about your competence. We're going to provide you with a systematic evaluation process that will determine whether you will remain as part of our faculty or will be asked to resign. At the same time, you will be receiving intensive assistance from a supervisor specifically designed to help you improve enough to remain with us. I sincerely hope that you will succeed.

In addition to orienting the teacher to the program, this initial taking-stock conference should also provide the teacher with an opportunity to identify specific changes the principal could make to provide greater support to the teacher. Doing so makes it clear that the teacher's classroom performance is affected by factors other than the characteristics and skill of the teacher.

Although such a discussion may easily turn into scapegoating and complaining, the principal can more productively give the session a problem-solving orientation. Thus, if the teacher complains about having unmotivated students, the principal can respond by asking, How can we work together to increase the motivation of students?

Such a conference might be held either at the end of the school year, as the culmination of a standard evaluation process, or at the beginning of the new school year when a new evaluation program is implemented. If held at the beginning of a school year, it should take place no later than mid-September.

Implement an
Intensive Evaluation Process

The principal should then implement the intensive evaluation process in a manner different in its details from the process used with the novice. Before the end of September, the principal should make the first observation, using whatever form the district provides. The observation should follow the guidelines provided in Chapter 3 for the evaluative observation. Note again that if the observation is to be unannounced then a preobservation conference should not be held.

That first observation should be followed by an evaluation conference in which the principal very directly assesses the quality of performance, providing specific data in support of each judgment. The principal should review the observation record and the evaluation report, giving the teacher an opportunity to add to both. The right of the teacher to add to the record is an important legal requirement that should be observed throughout the process.

The supervisor who is to provide the developmental services should be present at every taking-stock conference to ensure the close coordination of evaluation and development. However, as with the program for the novice, data generated by the supervisor about the success or failure of the teacher to profit from the developmental services should not become part of the evaluation record unless it is requested by the teacher.

The conference should conclude with the principal completing, with teacher input, a professional development plan that specifically indicates what skills need to be developed, how they will be developed, and who will provide the needed developmental services. Each participant—principal, teacher, and supervisor—should receive a copy.

The second observation and conference should follow closely on the heels of the first, probably early in October. By mid-October, the principal should hold a conference to evaluate the support skills, similar to the one held with the novice teacher. That conference should conclude with the completion of the form entitled *Professional Development Plan: Support Skills.*

By early November the principal should be ready to hold a second taking-stock conference: The supervisor should also participate in this conference. Together, they review the performance to date for the marginal teacher. If progress can already be seen, they may decide to slow up the pace of the evaluation process, while still continuing in the intensive mode. If no progress can be seen, they would continue to proceed at the scheduled pace.

Three additional observations with conferences would be held before the end of the first term: two before the winter break and one shortly after the break. A third taking-stock conference should be held at the end of the first semester. This is a crucial meeting in which the performance up to that time is assessed. The evaluation determines the overall quality of the teacher's performance. The principal should again be very direct in making the overall evaluation and providing evidence to support it, giving the teacher an opportunity to add to the record. At this time the principal should make one of three decisions with respect to the teacher's professional future: (a) the teacher will be retained because improvement has been made, (b) the teacher will be induced to resign, or (c) the principal will take formal action for dismissal. Two additional observations should be held in February and March, followed by a taking-stock conference in which the summative decision is implemented.

Throughout the entire process, the principal should also maintain an anecdotal record of the teacher's performance in noninstructional roles, such as supervising students before school, during lunch, during study periods, and after school. If the teacher does not perform such duties, performs them poorly, or performs them in an especially effective manner, the incident should be noted and described briefly.

Principals should keep in mind some guidelines as they carry out this evaluation program.

First, every observation and conference held and any assistance given should be documented. Second, the teacher should know at any given point how the principal assesses the performance. Third, the teacher should be given specific assistance to remedy deficiencies. Finally, the teacher should have an opportunity at any time to add comments to the official record, with the evaluation file available to the teacher at all times.

Providing this intensive evaluation to a marginal teacher is time-consuming and often emotionally taxing. However, the cost of keeping marginal teachers in the classroom is even higher.

Providing Intensive Development

As noted previously, the intensive evaluation needs to be supported with and accompanied by intensive development, preferably provided by a trained and certified supervisor. Although a peer mentor can usually be more effective than a central office supervisor in working with novices, a supervisor has the formal qualifications needed to support a negative evaluation of an experienced teacher if the matter is ever litigated. In small districts that lack central office supervisors or peer mentoring programs, an assistant principal or a principal from another school might be able to assist in providing intensive development, in that it is difficult for one principal to provide both evaluation and development.

Understand the Roots of Unsatisfactory Performance

Before discussing the specific developmental processes, it would be helpful to reflect about the nature of incompetence. The view advanced here is that the teacher's problems with specific instructional skills are rooted in some underlying causes; the observed deficiencies are the manifestations of some fundamental weaknesses. Those fundamental weaknesses seem to be of three sorts: (a) lack of general ability, (b) low motivation, and (c) counterproductive beliefs.

In that the problems of skill deficiency and low motivation are discussed elsewhere in this work, it would be especially useful here to examine more closely the counterproductive beliefs as they relate to the three types of marginal teachers identified earlier.

The wimp has never resolved the issue of power. Some wimps naively believe that students should have the power to determine what should happen in the classroom. Most lack a sense of efficacy, not believing in their own power. Some do not have enough confidence in themselves to use the power that inheres in the role. They are not sure how to assert themselves, coming across to the students as weak, uncertain, and timid. All these attitudes result in their inability and reluctance to use the formal power of the teacher's role in establishing a desirable learning environment. If the class is unruly because the teacher has failed to assert his or her authority, then the skills of explaining and questioning never have a fair chance to be used. Students respond to the wimp with disrespect and ridicule.

The martinet, on the other hand, is obsessed with power. Martinets want power over the classroom, ruling the classroom by establishing rigid rules and enforcing them with a heavy-handed discipline. They use the power of the reward system, using grades as rewards and punishments. They take off points from academic grades if students commit minor infractions. They even seem to enjoy their power to fail students, setting excessively high standards but providing little help to students who cannot meet them. This lust for power is accompanied by a lack of understanding of students, whom they tend to see as adversaries. Students respond to the martinet with fear or avoidance.

The basic problem with buddies is their seeming need for student affection. They use students to gratify their emotional needs because the adults in their lives are not responsive. This need for affection makes pleasing students their top priority: What do you want to study? What grade do you think you deserve? What activity pleases you? Buddies often single out a few students as the special objects of their affection. Students respond variously to buddies. Their favorites idolize them. The rest regard the buddy with a puzzled liking: Why does this adult want to be close to us?

Identifying and Dealing With the Root Cause

The preceding analysis suggests a somewhat complex developmental problem for the supervisor or the principal. The major task is to attempt to deal with the root cause, usually an attitudinal problem. The secondary task is to remedy the deficiencies growing out of the root cause. Both these tasks need to be accomplished in a relatively brief span of time—6 or 7 months, probably. Although such a complex endeavor cannot be reduced to a simple formula, the following approach has been found to be successful.

The developmental program should begin with an in-depth taking-stock conference of the supervisor and the teacher in September, following the meeting with the principal. The focus should be to enlist the marginal teacher in making a candid analysis of the problem by reflecting about its root causes. The following is how the supervisor might begin:

> As you are aware, you have been assigned to this special evaluation track. That means that the school administrators have serious questions about your performance. You probably disagree with those assessments, but that is not something I can control. I'll be working with you to help you improve in any skills where evaluators judge you to be unsatisfactory. But I would like to talk with you now about how you see the problem. What do you think are the underlying causes of the problems you are having in the classroom?

This discussion of root causes, which will probably require two or more separate sessions, will probably move through four related stages. The first stage is *supporting*. During this stage the goal is to strengthen the relationship by simply encouraging the teacher to reflect. The supervisor should be an active listener, paraphrasing and reflecting the teacher's perceptions. The second stage is *probing*. Now the supervisor asks questions designed to help the teacher move beyond a superficial analysis. The goal is to help the teacher look beneath the surface, again by reflecting about the cause beyond the cause. The following is an example:

Supervisor: What do you think is the root cause of your classroom management problems?

Teacher: The administration—they never follow through on discipline.

Supervisor: Let's grant for the time being that the administrators may be part of the problem. What part do you own?

The third stage is *data gathering*. At this stage, the supervisor and teacher will probably differ about the root cause. Rather than seeing the issue as a power struggle, they should move into a problem-solving mode. The data to be gathered will be from several sources: (a) a series of reflective journal entries by the teacher, (b) a survey of student perceptions, (c) the collaborative analysis of observational data and the professional development plan, and (d) the collaborative analysis of a videotape of the teacher in the classroom. The supervisor and the teacher should review the data in a cooperative spirit, trying to determine how the data reveal underlying difficulties. Neither is trying to prove that he or she was right; both are concerned instead with coming to a mutual understanding of the underlying issue.

The final stage is *reframing the problem*. The hope is that this extended process has enabled the teacher and the supervisor to agree on a redefinition of the underlying problem. At the outset, the teacher probably defined the problem in the following manner: I need to get greater support from the principal when I send students to the office. By the end of the reflective problem-solving process, the problem might be reframed as, I need to understand how to use my legitimate power to work with students in establishing a supportive learning environment.

Develop the Skills

If the above analysis is carried out in an insightful manner, using objective data, then the root cause can usually be linked with any deficiencies noted in the professional development plan. On those rare occasions when the root cause cannot be linked with the recommendations contained in the development plan, then the supervisor, with the permission of the teacher, should confer with the principal. The purpose of this session is to inform the principal of the results of the analysis and to recommend any modifications necessary in the professional development plan. Thus, two related objectives should be linked: the work on the root cause and implementation of the professional development plan with fidelity.

The specific services in implementing the development plan for the marginal teacher are generally similar to those provided to the

---

Specific Skills Involved in Classroom Management

The Presentation of Self

1. Speaks with a confident and firm tone of voice
2. Uses body language that projects a sense of confidence and self-assertiveness

Classroom Climate

3. Communicates very clear expectations with respect to a learning-centered climate
4. Establishes and communicates a clear set of rules and routines for classroom interactions
5. Structures the physical environment of the classroom so that environmental distractions are kept to a minimum

Planning for Instruction

6. Selects content and methods that will enable most students to achieve mastery with effort
7. Determines how to make the content meaningful to students
8. Chooses learning activities that will provide sufficient variety to sustain interest and achieve learning objectives
9. Establishes and implements an accountability system

Managing the Learning Task

10. Gives clear and explicit instructions
11. Monitors students as they work on the task
12. Uses the results of student work to monitor and adjust instruction
13. Continuously monitors all classroom interactions and behaviors in a way that does not interfere with teaching
14. Uses group alerting, asking all students to reflect about a question before identifying the one who is to answer

Dealing With Disruptive Behavior

15. Deals quietly and unobtrusively with minor infractions without embarrassing the student
16. Analyzes persistent problems of off-task behavior and, when necessary, enlists the help of parents and other professionals in dealing with them

---

novice. However, there are two differences that should be noted. First, the plan for the marginal teacher may require greater depth in that the problems are of long standing and are thus more deeply ingrained into the teacher's performance. For this reason, the supervisor may wish to begin the development with a fine-grained assessment. Consider, for example, the complex skills involved in establishing and maintaining a supportive learning environment, as shown in Box 6.2. Rather than talking generally about classroom discipline, the supervisor and teacher could make a specific assessment of which skills the teacher needs and which ones have the highest priority.

Second, the marginal teacher may require some professional counseling in dealing with long-standing attitudinal or personal problems. Although it is always a matter of some delicacy to suggest counseling, the teacher's need for help may be an overriding concern. The wimp may need some assertiveness training. The martinet may need the help of a therapist in examining the need for power. The buddy may need assistance in establishing productive adult relationships. Some school districts have organized employee assistance programs to help teachers secure such help.

Conclusion

In a given school, the problem of the marginal teacher may not seem significant in relation to the numbers involved. However, even one marginal teacher each year is interfering with the learning of 130 students, for one thirteenth of their public school experience. All principals, therefore, are encouraged to take the problem seriously and to act on it professionally.

7

Increasing Passive
Teachers' Motivation

Portrait of Tommy Jurgensen

Tommy Jurgensen has been teaching social studies for 15 years. He usually has been assigned low to average 9th and 10th graders. He is married to a woman who is very active in the local political party that has dominated all school board elections. They have no children.

Originally seen as a very promising young teacher, he seems now to have lost interest in teaching as a profession. Most of his energies—and time—are devoted to his growing insurance business. He has been very effective in developing his client base by contacting parents of all the students he teaches and boasts of the awards he has received from the insurance company.

There is no likelihood that he will be promoted to an administrative or supervisory role, and he feels cornered because of his insurance business.

Principal Alice Parpart is generally satisfied with his teaching. His students seem to perform well on the district's end-of-course tests, and there are no major problems with student discipline. However, she has become increasingly concerned with growing indications of Jurgensen's passivity. He spends a great deal of time having students practice on testlike items. In every formal observation, Parpart has noticed his strong reliance on the textbook and his excessive use of recitation and drill and practice. There was no evidence of systematic unit or lesson planning; the students themselves seemed very passive and unmotivated. The informal observations yielded similar results: Students were usually observed writing answers to textbook questions.

In the postobservation conferences, Jurgensen seemed to manifest an attitude of defensive compliance: "I get good test results, but I'll do what you tell me to do." His priorities are clearly elsewhere. He is usually the first to leave the building, often making excuses for not being able to attend departmental or faculty meetings, and seems simply to endure whatever staff development activities are provided. Students complain to the guidance counselor that he is rarely available for after-school help, and parents complain that they have difficulty contacting him. His response to such criticisms is always the same: "I give you my best during the hours the contract calls for; my personal time is my own."

* * *

The largest group of teachers who present special problems for the principal are teachers identified here as *passive*. Passive teachers are those who go through the motions of teaching, doing just as little as necessary to get by. Although they probably have mastered the basic skills, their motivation to teach is so low that at times they seem almost incompetent. This chapter analyzes the nature of the passive teacher and then suggests what can be done for the entire faculty and passive teachers to raise their level of motivation.

Understanding the Nature of the Passive Teacher

The passive teacher, as with all other teachers, is a unique individual whose special traits are often obscured by the general label. However, most exhibit the following characteristics:

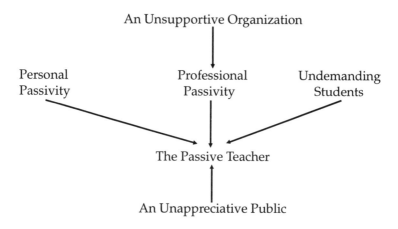

Figure 7.1. Factors Causing Teacher Passivity

- Their planning is minimal. They use the same plans from year to year. If they plan at all, they simply note the pages of the textbook they intend to use. They will submit lesson plans if required, but the plans are usually sketchy and unimaginative.
- Their teaching is passive. They spend most of class time having students complete workbook exercises. Their body language and their voice suggest clearly to the students that they are not enthusiastic about the curriculum, teaching, or the students.
- Their tests emphasize rote learning. They rely chiefly on multiple choice and true-false questions, in that such items are easiest to score.
- Their participation in school governance and student activities is sufficient only to satisfy administrative requirements. They are usually the first teachers to leave the building. They sit passively at faculty meetings counting the minutes until the meeting is ended.
- Their professional growth is almost nonexistent. Satisfied with their present level of competence, they see no need to take graduate courses (except to get certificates that will enable them to escape the classroom) or to participate voluntarily in faculty workshops.

- They tolerate supervision as a necessary evil. In that they can usually demonstrate the basic skills when an observer is present, they almost always receive *satisfactory* ratings. They see the supervisory conference as a charade in which they play a stereotyped role. If the principal makes a suggestion for improvement, their standard response is, "That's a good idea—I'll try that in the next unit—thanks a lot." Most have no intention of carrying through.

What factors account for teacher passivity? As indicated in Figure 7.1, there are two factors external to the school and three internal ones.

External Factors

The first external factor is an *unappreciative public*. All teachers want to believe that they are valued by the public. If the public are unappreciative of the demands of teaching and are highly critical of the schools, teachers are less likely to be motivated to teach. This presents an interesting paradox. When parents were asked to rate the schools their oldest child attended, 70% gave those schools a grade of A or B (Elam, Rose, & Gallup, 1994). However, when asked by the same pollsters to rate the nation's schools, only 22% gave a grade of A or B. The impact of such ratings is underscored by Carson, Huelskamp, and Woodall (1992): "The combination of the low status of educators and a lack of confidence from the public may paint a bleak picture for the future. It raises the specter of a downward spiral in future educational quality" (p. 291).

The second external factor is what is termed here as *personal passivity*, defined as those elements of the teacher as a person, outside the school setting, that seem to account for passive behavior. Several elements operate here. If the teacher is an unassertive and dependent individual because of innate traits, learned behavior, or environmental factors, that lack of assertiveness and dependency will likely carry over to the classroom. If the teacher has major health problems that result in low energy levels and chronic pain, the teacher brings that listlessness and pain to the classroom. If the teacher plays several roles other than the professional one, the resulting overload means that less time and energy are available for teaching. Most teachers have families to take care of, many are enrolled in graduate courses, and a large percentage hold part-time jobs.

Although these external factors lie beyond the direct control of the principal, it is useful for the principal to understand the existence of those factors and attempt to minimize their power. To counteract the negative messages from the public, the principal can work with the faculty and the parent-teacher organization to plan and implement a comprehensive project for developing public appreciation for the schools. That project should first involve a public relations campaign that disseminates accurate information about the success of public schools in general and the accomplishments of the local school more specifically. The success of the public schools is well documented in Bracey (1994) and Carson et al. (1992). The project should also include a Teacher Appreciation Day, in which community leaders and parents pay special tribute to the work of teachers. Finally, the principal should speak often to the public and to the faculty of the accomplishments of the school and the contributions of the teachers. Too often reform efforts are directed solely to what the schools are doing wrong.

To counteract the negative impact of the personal elements, the principal can tactfully explore with the teacher the extent to which those elements are influencing classroom behavior and provide whatever support is needed. These personal factors are delicate matters that involve the teacher's personal need for privacy and should be examined only if the teacher indicates a willingness to do so.

Internal Factors

The internal factors are those within the school that account for teacher passivity. Three sets are identified here: (a) an unsupportive organization, (b) undemanding students, and (c) professional passivity.

An Unsupportive Organization. If the organization is structured in a manner that does not support good teaching, then faculty motivation in general will be low. Making the organization a supportive environment for quality teaching should have a perceptible effect on all teachers, not just the passive ones. As Johnson (1990) points out, the public cannot expect talented teachers to serve selflessly in schools that discourage their best efforts.

Undemanding Students. Undemanding students can also inhibit the motivation of teachers. If students have low expectations, want to avoid hard work, and challenge teachers who demand too much of them, then such behaviors reinforce teacher passivity. One researcher notes that sometimes teachers attempt to achieve order in the classroom by selecting only those tasks that are familiar and easy for students (Doyle, 1986).

Professional Passivity. Professional passivity denotes those aspects of the teacher as a professional that contribute toward teacher passivity. Note that the key elements of professional passivity identified following are chiefly components of the teacher's belief system.

- The teacher believes that teaching is just another job, with no special meaning or significance.
- The teacher believes that the district owes him or her a specified number of absences for illness or personal reasons, thus leading to a high number of teacher absences.
- The teacher believes that he or she cannot reach students or make a difference in their knowledge and attitudes.
- The teacher believes that some students are just incapable of learning.
- The teacher's goals are vague, idiosyncratic, and easy to achieve.
- The teacher focuses on the extrinsic rewards of teaching—long summer vacations, short hours, and frequent vacations.
- The teacher discredits the value of feedback and does not solicit feedback from students, other teachers, parents, and administrators. The teacher responds with denial and defensiveness to any negative feedback.
- The teacher believes that he or she has very little autonomy, complaining frequently about state and district policies and principal regulations.

Thus, the passive teacher is caught in a cycle of defeatism. He or she holds negative beliefs about self, teaching, and students; those negative beliefs lead to passive unmotivated teaching. That kind of teaching alienates students and diminishes their capacity to learn.

Their negative attitudes and problems in learning reinforce the teacher's negativism and passivity.

Defeating Teacher Passivity

One of the most awesome challenges facing principals is defeating teacher passivity. For this complex task, there are no quick fixes or easy answers. However, a review of the research and reflection about the authors' experience suggest that three general strategies can have an ameliorating effect: (a) strengthening the organization as a supportive work environment, (b) shaping teacher beliefs through staff development, and (c) helping individual teachers become more powerful. Principals are encouraged to review these strategies, adapting them for their schools and using them flexibly.

Strengthening the Organization as a Supportive Work Environment

The first approach is designed to impact on the entire faculty by strengthening the school's work environment. Rather than advocating a comprehensive restructuring of the schools, the position advanced here is one of incremental change. In this incremental model, the goal is to maintain and reinforce the desirable elements that are already present, while identifying and strengthening one or two priority elements that need changing.

The process begins with a simple assessment. Using a survey form similar to the one shown in Box 7.1, the leadership team would assess teachers' perceptions of the work environment. Average or mean scores can easily be computed by equating each response with a number: 4 (*strongly agree*) to 1 (*strongly disagree*). The team can then analyze the results, using the following guidelines:

Scores 3.5 to 4.0: Organizational strengths that need to be maintained

Scores 2.5 to 3.4: Ambiguities that need probing

Scores 1.0 to 2.4: Perceived weaknesses that need to be strengthened

---

BOX 7.1

Assessing the School as a Work Environment

Directions. Consider each of the statements below as it presently applies to our school. Indicate the extent to which you agree or disagree with that statement as it presently applies to our school: SA *(strongly agree)*, A *(agree)*, D *(disagree)*, or SD *(strongly disagree)*.

1. Our faculty generally believe that student learning is our highest priority.
2. Our faculty are vitally concerned with their own professional growth and development.
3. Teachers and administrators work collaboratively and cooperatively for school improvement.
4. The principal treats teachers with the professional respect they deserve.
5. Parents have a high regard for teaching as a profession and respect the professionalism of our faculty.
6. The principal and teachers share a common vision for the school and work toward shared goals.
7. The school is a safe and orderly environment for teaching.
8. Teachers are provided with adequate resources to do their job.
9. The principal is a dynamic leader who works with teachers for continuous improvement.
10. Teachers are actively involved in making decisions that affect their teaching.
11. Our school emphasizes productivity and accomplishment.
12. In our school, good teaching is recognized and rewarded.
13. Quality time is provided teachers to plan and collaborate on professional projects.
14. Teachers have sufficient autonomy with respect to what they teach and how they teach.
15. Teachers have teachable assignments: Classes are not too large, too disruptive, or too demanding in their diversity.
16. Teachers receive timely and constructive feedback from colleagues.
17. Teachers receive timely and constructive feedback from administrators and supervisors.
18. Considering everything, this school provides a supportive environment for quality teaching.

The principal can then ask each team or department to discuss more fully the "ambiguities," which represent areas in which there is no clear agreement. The results of those discussions should determine whether an item represents a potential strength that may need some work or a potential weakness that needs improvement.

The team should then rank order the perceived weaknesses to identify one component that meets these criteria:

Is generally perceived as a weakness

Is an important aspect of the environment from the perspective of that school

Can be changed without requiring an excessive amount of resources

The intent is to identify one change that the faculty can bring about successfully in their first effort to improve the organization.

With that one priority change identified, the team can then use an action research approach in studying and solving the problem. The following, for example, is an action research plan for dealing with Item 5 in the survey: "Parents have a high regard for teaching as a profession and respect the professionalism of our faculty."

1. The leadership team meets with PTO officers to establish a joint task force to study the issue and develop a solution.
2. The task force surveys and interviews parents to understand the nature and extent of the problem.
3. The task force reviews the research on developing positive parent attitudes toward teachers.
4. The task force develops an intervention plan based on their study of the problem and their knowledge of the research.
5. The principal submits intervention plans to the PTO and the faculty for their review and modification.
6. The leadership team implements and evaluates the final intervention plan.

Obviously the final plan would provide greater detail about the specifics and timing of the interventions.

Shaping Teacher Beliefs Through Staff Development

The second intervention strategy is to impact on teacher beliefs that are related to professional passivity. The optimal approach is to work with the entire faculty in a series of sessions devoted to the issue. Rather than isolating and stigmatizing those who are judged to be passive, the principal will be more effective by involving the entire faculty. If only the passive are brought together, they will reinforce each other in their negativism. Motivated teachers can be very effective in influencing the passive ones.

How these sessions are organized and structured is a matter for the leadership team to resolve. Some principals have found it effective to devote part of each faculty meeting to a discussion of the issues; others have met with teams and departments for a series of discussions; still others have organized a special series of staff development sessions.

Regardless of the structure used, principals should keep in mind that beliefs can be changed through increased knowledge, reflection, and interaction with respected peers. An effective program will include components such as (a) assessing present beliefs and finding a focus, (b) acquiring empirical knowledge, (c) discerning personal knowledge, (d) learning from the personal knowledge of others, (e) identifying discrepant beliefs, (f) testing discrepant beliefs, and (g) reaching a tentative closure.

The following discussion examines how this model could be implemented. The process begins with an assessment of faculty attitudes with respect to the beliefs noted previously. Here again a survey is the simplest means of making such a determination. A form similar to the one shown in Box 7.2 can be used to assess faculty beliefs. The results can be used to identify one belief that could profitably be examined. The recommendation is that the process should begin by examining one key belief about which there is significant difference among the faculty. The intent is to begin with one belief that is held by a majority of the faculty but questioned by a substantial minority. Such a belief would be easier to change than one not held by a large majority.

The principal can then plan and implement one or more sessions devoted to an examination of the belief selected for examination. A process similar to the one described in the following can be used (the description assumes that a belief in teacher efficacy has been selected for analysis).

First, prior to the meeting, the workshop leader distributes a two-page handout that defines *teacher efficacy* and reviews the research

---

BOX 7.2

Survey of Teacher Beliefs

Directions. Consider each statement below. Indicate the extent to which you agree or disagree with that statement.

1. Teaching is an important profession, not just another job.
2. I know that I have the power to reach all students.
3. I believe that all students can achieve the learning goals of our school, if they have good teaching and the right support.
4. I have very clear goals for my teaching that are shared by my colleagues.
5. The best part of being a teacher is knowing that I am making a difference with my students.
6. I value feedback from colleagues.
7. I value feedback from students.
8. I value feedback from supervisors and administrators.
9. I have sufficient autonomy with respect to what I teach and how I teach it.

---

on its importance. Providing these background materials in print form reduces the need for lecture. The session begins with a brief review of the handout and an opportunity for the participants to ask questions to clarify any points that confuse them.

Next, the participants are given 10 minutes to write their individual answer to the question, What have I learned from my teaching experience about teacher efficacy? The writing process is a useful means of discerning personal knowledge, the knowledge that comes from experience.

The third step is to divide the participants into small discussion groups of five to six members. If possible, the small groups should be structured so that each group includes several teachers who hold the belief and a few who disagree. The leader asks each person to take no more than 5 minutes to share his or her personal knowledge about teacher efficacy. The leader stresses the importance of active listening, not argumentation. The sharing of personal knowledge is intended to foster understanding of each other's perspective, not to vote on which point of view is right. After each person has made a brief presentation, the leader leads a discussion that attempts to identify areas of agreement and issues that need further exploration. The process is intended to raise questions in the minds of participants about negative beliefs that are inhibiting productive behavior.

The leader of each group then presents a brief report to the entire faculty, identifying areas of agreement and issues that need further examination. Based on those final reports, the principal summarizes, as in the following example:

> We seem to agree about two major beliefs. We agree that there are forces that limit our power, chiefly the degree of family support and the amount of peer influence. But we also agree that we must believe in our power to make some difference with most of our students. Not believing in our own power is a self-fulfilling prophecy. We seem to disagree about whether there are a few students who are just beyond our reach. That is an important issue that needs further testing and discussion.

What is the effect of such a program on passive teachers who doubt their efficacy? They have acquired new knowledge that challenges their beliefs. They have had an opportunity to discern and articulate their personal knowledge. They have listened to respected peers who differ with them. They now have some doubts about those cherished beliefs. And they know that they are part of an organization in which differences are respected, principles matter, and positive thinking is valued. They have not been converted, only challenged.

Helping Individual Teachers Become More Productive

The final phase of the program turns to work with individual teachers who seem passive. The process begins with the principal conferring with a teacher whom the principal has so identified. Rather than labeling the teacher *passive* or *unmotivated*, the principal identifies specific behaviors that are a concern. The following is an example:

> I want to discuss candidly with you some aspects of your teaching that concern me. Before discussing my concerns, I should make it clear that I do not consider you an unsatisfactory

teacher; I believe you have mastered the essential skills. Let me identify some specific behaviors that lead me to wonder about what is happening with you. Then I would like to give you an opportunity to share your own perceptions. First, your planning does not seem to be highly professional. Your unit plans are often very sketchy and seem to rely a great deal on the text. Second, when I make my informal observations, your students are typically engaged in seat work, while you sit at your desk scoring tests or checking your notes. Finally, I have seen no evidence that you are trying to develop yourself as a professional. How do you see these matters?

Notice that the principal begins by being very direct about the focus of the discussion. Next the principal allays the teacher's anxieties about the overall evaluation. Then the principal describes specific indicators that suggest passivity. The principal concludes this opening statement by giving the teacher an opportunity to respond.

The principal needs to be prepared for one of four responses the teacher might make, with the principal answering appropriately, as follows.

1. The teacher denies the evidence: "You just haven't seen my best plans or my best teaching." The principal indicates that the difference of opinion will be resolved through additional observation.

2. The teacher admits the evidence but offers excuses: "My wife is sick." "I'm not feeling well." "Too much is on my mind." The principal expresses empathy but makes it clear that productive teaching is expected regardless of those excuses.

3. The teacher admits the evidence but blames others: "I have very difficult classes." "My team leader doesn't help me." The principal agrees to work together on problems that might exist, but holds the teacher accountable for productive teaching.

4. The teacher admits the evidence and agrees to make the needed changes. The principal praises the professional response and offers to assist.

Whatever responses the teacher makes, the principal directs the discussion so that it focuses on future actions that will be taken by both. In general, the following plan should be implemented.

First, they agree that for the time being the teacher will remain on the standard evaluation track unless there seems to be no change in behavior. If the principal believes that the motivation is so low that it results in unacceptable behavior or if the principal sees no signs of improvement, then the teacher should be moved to the intensive evaluation track.

Second, they agree that the teacher will play an active role as a member of a cooperative development team. It is hoped that the pressure of productive peers will increase the teacher's motivation. If the teacher is vehement about wanting to work in a self-directed mode, the principal may decide to agree as long as there is evidence of progress.

Next, they agree on specific actions that the teacher will take to remedy specific problems. Thus, if one of the indicators is poor planning, then they might agree that the teacher would work with a peer in developing quality units, to be reviewed by the principal. Finally, all these decisions are formalized into a professional development plan that the teacher and the principal can use in assessing progress.

Conclusion

Passive and unmotivated teachers should not be tolerated in that they represent a significant waste of resources. The combination of strengthening the organization, shaping teacher beliefs, and helping individual teachers should make a significant difference in those who have just been getting by with minimal effort. Principals also need to model positive attitudes and behaviors for these teachers and demonstrate consistently the belief that all teachers can improve with appropriate assistance. Passive teachers tend to be cynical and quickly note inconsistencies in a principal's behavior.

Fostering the Growth
of Nonteaching Staff

A lmost all the books on supervision concern themselves solely with the supervision of teachers, ignoring two very important groups—the nonteaching professionals and the classified staff. Both groups play a part in the success of the school and should be included in the principal's plans for improving learning. This chapter includes an extended discussion of how the growth of nonteaching professionals can be fostered and concludes with an examination of the development of classified staff.

The Role Priorities
for Nonteaching Professionals

Nonteaching professionals include counselors, nurses, librarians (or library media specialists, as they are sometimes called), and social workers. (Throughout this chapter, they will be identified as *special staff*.) In some school districts, these special staff members are evaluated and supervised by a central office administrator or supervisor; in others, the principal evaluates and supervises them. Regardless of the administrative organization, there is much that the principal can do to foster the professional development and use the talents of such personnel. These professionals represent a significant resource often overlooked by principals with a narrow vision of the concept of *faculty*, equating faculty with classroom teachers.

First, the principal should ensure that the special staff have a clear understanding of their role and know which functions should receive top priority. The importance of role clarity is indicated by research that concluded that administrators and counselors misunderstood how each perceived the counselor's role (Stickel, 1990).

If no official role description exists, the principal should work with those professionals (along with any responsible central office administrator) to develop a role definition that also indicates role priorities. An example of such a description for a counselor is shown in Box 8.1. Such a role description should facilitate communication between the principal and the staff member with respect to how the staff member allocates time; it should also ameliorate the problem of frequently expecting the staff member to take on additional responsibilities without providing assistance or modifying the role definition.

Develop and Implement
Policies of Inclusiveness

One of the best ways of fostering the professional development of special staff is to develop and implement a policy of inclusiveness that makes them a vital part of the faculty. The school nurse who is never included in faculty activities and is never recognized feels isolated and unappreciated and loses contact with the teachers.

The principal can accomplish this goal in several ways. First, the principal should use all appropriate occasions to emphasize their importance, to acknowledge their contributions, and to use their special

---

BOX 8.1

Role of High School Counselors

The following specifications indicate the functions that counselors are expected to perform. The percentage figure in parentheses suggests the relative emphasis that should be given to that function.

With Students

1. Collect, maintain, and input accurate information for student records, giving major attention to students with special needs (5%)
2. Counsel individual students and groups of students with respect to their program planning and scheduling, their academic and interpersonal problems, and their plans for careers and higher education (30%)
3. Assist students in gaining admission to higher education, finding jobs, and identifying special learning opportunities outside of school (10%)
4. Coordinate the provision of other professional services (such as those of the school psychologist and the school social worker) when necessary (5%)

With the Teachers

5. Communicate with teachers about students who are experiencing difficulty (10%)
6. Work with teachers in a problem-solving approach to improve learning for students (10%)

With the Administrators and the School in General

7. Identify general teaching-learning problems as they emerge from individual and group counseling (10%)
8. Assist with the development of student schedules (5%)
9. Conduct research on the success of graduates and the effectiveness of school programs (5%)

With Parents

10. Communicate with parents and, when necessary, coordinate the parent communication of other professionals (10%)

---

talents. They should play an active role in all faculty committees and activities. Pickard (1993) points out, for example, that the library media specialist can serve as an "instructional consultant," helping teachers identify, locate, evaluate, and apply learning resources. Most important, they should be included as active members of the instructional teams.

In larger schools where there are several special staff members of each type, each special staff member should be assigned to one of the instructional teams, to ensure that he or she feels included and to provide systematic opportunities for input. If there is only one counselor, for example, then the principal should work with that individual to build a schedule that ensures systematic contact with all teams.

Foster Growth Through
Self-Directed Development

In fostering the professional development of these special staff members, it is recommended that they participate in the self-directed approach in that the skills they need to develop are so highly specialized. Special staff members who wish to be involved in the cooperative mode with an instructional team should, of course, be encouraged to do so as a means of complementing their work in the self-directed mode.

As explained in Chapter 3, the self-directed mode operates as follows. The staff member in conference with the principal sets a professional development goal for the year, preferably linking that goal with the school improvement plan. In that initial conference, they also agree as to how the goal will be accomplished and how progress will be assessed. The principal confers at least once with the staff member to assess progress and once to determine the summative evaluation.

Structure Opportunities
for Faculty Interaction

In addition to working with groups of teachers, these special staff members should be expected to work with the entire faculty by participating actively in faculty meetings and playing a significant role in staff development. For example, in a staff development program to improve student motivation, the school nurse could contribute by providing the teachers with information about the health factors that lead to low motivation to learn.

Monitor the Performance
of Special Staff

The principal should monitor the performance of these special staff members, even if their formal evaluation is the responsibility of central office personnel. The monitoring can usually be accomplished by making the same kind of informal observations that are recommended for classrooms; the only caution, of course, is that the principal should never intrude on private conferences that the staff member is holding with students.

Help Special Staff Members
Use Student Feedback

As explained earlier, teachers can profit from student feedback. Such feedback is perhaps even more important for the special staff in that they lack most of the other sources of feedback available to teachers: They do not give tests, and they do not usually have a peer or supervisor observe them at work. A simple feedback form such as the one shown in Box 8.2 can be used, for example, in helping the school nurse.

Meet Periodically
With Special Staff

One of the most productive ways of fostering the growth of special staff is to meet with them on a scheduled basis. Such meetings should begin by giving them time to identify any problems they perceive from their special perspective. The principal can then help the group classify the problems into one of three categories, as follows:

- Simple problems that are easy to solve and can be dealt with at once. The high school librarian asks for a special budget allocation for current teenage fiction dealing with special-needs youth. The principal decides to request the parent organization to use part of its budget. The principal uses the occasion to remind the

---

BOX 8.2

Student Feedback to School Nurse

Directions. Our school nurse, Ms. Williams, is interested in learning how students evaluate the services she provides. Your responses will help her do a better job.

First, indicate here how often you have met with her so far this year as part of a group or as an individual: _____

Next, indicate to what extent you agree or disagree with the statement: SA (*strongly agree*), A (*agree*), D (*disagree*), or SD (*strongly disagree*).

Ms. Williams . . .

1. Has helped me when I did not feel well
2. Has given me good information about how to stay healthy
3. Knows how to make the school a healthful environment
4. Has kept my parents informed about my health problems
5. Is easy to talk with and understands young people
6. Is known and liked by most of the students

---

special staff of the need to keep regular students sensitive to the feelings of handicapped students who have been included in regular classes.

- Ambiguous problems of moderate complexity that require additional data before a decision is made. Suppose, for example, that one of the elementary counselors has become aware of some bullying taking place after school while students are waiting for school buses. After some discussion, the group decides to get additional data from teachers to determine if the problem is a major one affecting the whole school or whether it is localized to a few students who need to be dealt with individually. The principal leads the group in a brief discussion of the root causes of bullying behavior.

- Problems so complex and significant that they need to be addressed through in-depth problem solving. The school nurse in a middle school expresses a concern that most students seem unaware of the dangers of excessive fat in the diet. The counselor agrees, noting that students often talk about stopping at the neighborhood convenience store for fatty snacks. The school social worker expresses a concern that parents seem unaware of the nutritional needs of young adolescents. A preliminary analysis of the curriculum indicates that good nutrition is not included in the middle school curriculum. The group decide to recommend to the School Improvement Team that a systematic study of the problem be undertaken. The principal points out that complex problems of this sort often involve the parents, the school, and social service agencies in a collaborative effort. The observation leads to a discussion of the need for improved collaboration.

The examples indicate the critical nature of such meetings: They provide an opportunity for special staff to identify problems; they enable the principal to do some informal staff development; and they underscore the significance of cooperation between special staff, administrators, and classroom teachers.

Foster Growth
of Classified Staff

Other nonteaching employees whose professional development needs to be considered are the classified staff. Classified employees have a significant impact on the success of the school in its day-to-day operations and in the effectiveness of home-school relationships. Their professional development should not be overlooked. Several strategies can work here.

First, provide or arrange for special workshops that keep them up to date with respect to their areas of responsibility. For example, school bus drivers need to have special instruction about new equipment, new rules of student conduct, and new transportation routes.

Second, ensure that the classified staff are kept informed about professional matters. It usually is a good idea to have one secretary attend faculty meetings and then inform the rest of the classified staff. Keeping the classified staff informed is an effective way of reducing the spread of ill-founded rumors.

Finally, meet with the classified staff on a regular basis. One principal we know hires two secretarial substitutes for 2 hours each month, so that he can meet with classified staff to discuss problems from their perspective.

Conclusion

These nonteaching professionals and classified staff can make a major contribution to the overall welfare of the student body and the general effectiveness of the school. To optimize their effectiveness, the principal needs to implement a policy of inclusiveness and to use strategies that will foster their professional growth.

Support Resources
for Professional Growth

Even the most effective principal cannot accomplish these complex tasks of professional development alone. Wise principals will build supportive constituencies and use current technology to foster teacher development in the most effective manner.

Building Board and
Superintendent Support

The types of teacher development programs come about in three different ways. In some cases, the central administration of the school district develops a comprehensive district approach, which typically gives individual schools some latitude in the details of implementation. Some of these alternative programs are adopted as a component of a systematic school-based management program. Finally, some schools have simply become dissatisfied with standard supervisory approaches and, with superintendent approval, develop their own approach to teacher development.

Regardless of the genesis of the program, the principal needs to work closely with the superintendent, who in turn can keep the school board informed and can determine if any direct contact between the board and the principal is needed. Principals report that the following strategies have been effective.

First, be sure that any program conforms with the provisions of school law, school board policy, and the teachers' contract. As explained in Chapter 3, those responsible for developing the program should begin by checking these constraints. If the analysis of board policies identifies some major constraints that might inhibit program effectiveness, the principal should confer with the superintendent to determine if the policy might be modified.

Next, involve the superintendent early in the development of the program. Superintendents will vary in the extent to which they should be involved; however, they should all be viewed as a valuable resource. The principal should keep the superintendent fully informed at every major stage in the process of developing a new program for teacher development and should seek the superintendent's input into significant aspects of the new program.

Third, be sure to get the superintendent's support for any special resources needed. This support is especially critical at budget-making time. If the new program is to be effective, it will need time, money, and materials.

As the program is introduced and initially implemented, be sure to acknowledge the superintendent's contribution. Contrast the impact of the following two news releases on the extent to which the superintendent will feel disposed to support the program:

Principal-Centered

Central Middle School, under the leadership of its principal Susan Armbruster, is introducing this year a new program designed to improve teaching. Armbruster emphasized the importance of the program in improving student learning . . .

Superintendent-Centered

Joan Rodriguez, superintendent of the Union School District, announced yesterday that the school district will be embarking on a new program designed to improve student learning by improving teaching. The first version of the new approach will be piloted at the Central Middle School, under the leadership of Principal Susan Armbruster.

Finally, keep the superintendent informed about the progress of the program. Most principals, understandably, are eager to let the superintendent know of the success of the program. It is even more important to alert the superintendent to major problems that may be emerging. One basic rule of the principalship is: *Never let the superintendent be surprised by bad news that comes from some other source.*

Working With Other Principals

In too many instances, principals see each other as competitors. They compete for public attention, board and superintendent approval, and scarce resources. Most of this competition is counterproductive in that it leads to divisiveness, fragmentation of the district's mission, and isolation of each school. If cooperation is good for students and for teachers, then it is also good for principals.

Such cooperation takes many forms. Principals should exchange ideas and share successful practices with each other, especially in the initial stages of program development. Such open sharing of ideas can strengthen all programs and make them much less insular in approach. If regular contact with other principals is lacking, discuss with the superintendent the importance of such relationships for teachers and students and explore how they can be strengthened.

Principals can also work together to foster each other's professional development. Projects that structure collaborative learning for principals report success in providing such activities among principal-peers as shadowing each other, observing the principal's behavior in conducting meetings, observing a class together and sharing insights, and debriefing each other (see, e.g., Barnett, 1990). The principal of another school in the district can also perform a very useful service in performing evaluation observations of a marginal teacher in a colleague's school, if district policies and contracts permit such activity.

Principals can also emphasize teacher cooperation across the district. They should encourage teacher leaders from each participating school to meet together to share experiences and insights. They should arrange for teachers to observe colleagues with similar teaching assignments in other schools in the district. Such observations of peers should be carefully structured so that they have a developmental, not an evaluative, focus and a clear purpose to avoid being aimless.

Using Central Office Staff Effectively

The central office supervisor can also be a very helpful resource for these new approaches to teacher development. However, some changes will have to occur if these supervisors are to offer constructive assistance. The research on the impact of central office supervisors suggests that their present mode of functioning has minimal influence on the classroom teacher. Glatthorn (in press) concludes his review of the research by noting that the teacher tends to perceive the district supervisor as a somewhat remote and relatively unhelpful professional who gives most attention to maintaining the system as it is, rather than reforming it.

The way the supervisor is used in these programs will obviously be affected by district role descriptions and supervisory practices. However, reports from successful programs suggest the following general guidelines for practice.

First, involve the supervisors in the design and development of the school's program. They can bring to bear some useful insights from the district perspective and can suggest ways of adapting the recommendations of this book to the special context of that school district.

Next, work with the supervisors to clarify the role they can best play for each group of teachers. The role definition can be developed systematically by (a) reviewing district policies and role descriptions, (b) assessing the competence and availability of supervisors, (c) analyzing school-based resources, and (d) determining how central office supervisors can best complement school-based resources. Although

BOX 9.1

Supervisor Schedule, Central High School

Supervisor and Area: Harrison Tompkins, Mathematics
Principal: Allan Smithton
Month: October

Tentative Date	Group or Individual	Purpose
2nd	McCracken	Diagnostic observation and debriefing
5th	McCracken	Coaching based on diagnosis
9th	Math department	New standards from NCTM and their implications
12th	Principal's cabinet	Current research in teaching problem solving
12th	McCracken	Focused observation

this analysis will give varying results from school to school, the special skills and experience of these supervisors make them uniquely qualified to provide intensive development services to marginal teachers. If district policies permit, they can also serve as an external evaluator in the intensive evaluation component.

Next, collaborate with the supervisors to develop a monthly schedule based on the results of that role analysis. The schedule should be specific with respect to how many visits the supervisor will make and the purpose of each visit. An example of such a schedule is shown in Box 9.1.

Finally, use the supervisor to assist in the evaluation of the program. As someone external to the school, the supervisor is likely to be more objective in assessing the program's strengths and weaknesses.

Collaborating With Universities

One of the encouraging results of the movement to reform teacher education is an emphasis on collaboration between universities and schools. In some cases, this collaboration takes the form of selecting certain schools as "professional development schools," where much of the preservice training takes place (Levine, 1992). Even where such structured relationships do not exist, principals should make systematic use of university resources when they are available.

First, identify a knowledgeable faculty member who is a specialist in supervision as a consultant to the program. That specialist can bring an external perspective to program development, can assist in program design and evaluation, and can share the results of current research that has implications for the program.

Second, consider using university faculty members as external evaluators in the intensive evaluation program. As noted previously, an external evaluator can be a very useful adjunct to school administrators in evaluating teacher effectiveness.

The training of student teachers should be closely integrated with the school's professional development program, rather than being seen as an extraneous element. School-based mentors can assume much of the supervision of student teachers, if they are given the needed training and time to do the job (see University of North Carolina, 1992). If this occurs, then the university supervisors can focus on the evaluation of student teachers. Skilled university supervisors can also be used effectively in the development of novice teachers, to ensure a smooth transition from preservice to inservice development.

Involving Parents and the Community

Both parents and the general public will need to be educated about the nature of the program and kept informed about its progress, so that they become supporters of the program at budget-making time. In accomplishing this goal, principals should keep in mind certain basic precepts of effective school-community relationships. First, do not oversell the program before it is implemented. Many parents and other community members have become cynical about educational innovations because they have been oversold as final solutions to complex problems.

Also, when informing the lay public, emphasize the impact of the program on student learning. In doing so, do not use educational jargon and do not write or speak in a condescending manner. The following, for example, is how a principal might explain *intensive development* to a parent organization:

We are using a new approach to helping our first-year teachers refine their skills. We're also using this new approach with a small number of experienced teachers who seem to need special help. We feel sure that this new program will result in better teaching, which will mean better learning. We're going to assign them a highly skilled teacher or supervisor as a mentor to work closely with them. That mentor will observe their teaching several times each term, will discuss the lesson with them, and will give them special coaching in the skills they need to acquire. We will keep you posted about the progress of the program.

Also, in all press releases and group presentations, emphasize the positive aspects of the program, rather than calling undue attention to the passive or marginal teachers.

Principals should be honest with the public in acknowledging that, as in any profession, some teachers are not quite as competent as they should be and some need a "shot in the arm." However, these groups should not be the focus of public attention.

Finally, where there are major corporations in the community, their training experts can often be useful in emphasizing to the public the importance of continuing staff development and training and in sharing with program leaders insights they have gained in employee training.

Using the Technology

In addition to these human resources, principals should also make effective use of the technology to foster teachers' professional development. The final section of this book, "Additional Resources," lists several multimedia resources that should be useful. Two special uses of the technology need more careful examination.

Computers as an Observation Tool

Some principals report the effective use of the laptop computer as an observational tool (Kuralt, 1987). The advantages of using the computer are that (a) it is a more efficient note-taking tool, (b) with the appropriate software, the data can be analyzed readily from several perspectives, and (c) it provides a fully documented record for the principal and the teacher. There are, however, some drawbacks in that it can seem intrusive to both teachers and students and its use may take the principal's eyes away from critical interactions.

Videotapes for Analysis

Reports from those using camcorders to make videotapes of teaching indicate that the analysis of such tapes is a valuable experience. The following benefits are reported in the literature: (a) teachers concentrate on their teaching when they analyze such tapes, (b) the videotapes create a valuable record of teaching, (c) the feedback from the video validates observer feedback, (d) viewing demonstrations by peers helps teachers solve instructional problems, (e) peer discussion focusing on the videos strengthens collegiality, and (f) the video analysis facilitates the coaching process (see Rogers, 1987). The explanation that follows clarifies how to make a videotape of teaching and how to analyze the tape.

Making the Videotape. The principal should first train the teachers in how to make videotapes, following these guidelines.

1. Choose a class that will provide a supportive context for their teaching. That does not mean that teachers necessarily choose the most able; instead, it suggests that teachers select a class that will be responsive and not disruptive.
2. Prepare the class. In that some students will find the camera intrusive, prepare them for being taped. Explain the purpose of the taping and solicit their cooperation. One teacher who frequently makes videotapes reports that it helps to have the camera set up in the classroom several days before the taping; in that way, the students become used to its presence.
3. Prepare the equipment and the personnel. Be sure the camera is operating well, with the right kind of tape. Teachers can (a) mount the camera in a stationary manner and simply turn it on and off (the least satisfactory), (b) train a student, or (c) ask for

---

BOX 9.2

Videotape: Running Record

Tape Counter	Teacher Actions	Student Actions
52	Checking roll	All but 3 are working on sponge activity

---

the assistance of an aide or colleague. Depending on the information desired from the videotape, the camera might be focused on the students' interactions instead of the teacher's behaviors.

4. Make several tapes. Making several tapes will allow the students to become used to the camera, teachers to select the tape that best suits their purposes, teachers to have backup tapes in case the one selected becomes damaged or lost. If teachers decide to make several tapes, they should consider making them all for the same unit, one each from the beginning, middle, and end of the unit. Some experts recommend that teachers leave the camcorder in the classroom for several periods and make many informal tapes before they make the official one (Eckart & Gibson, 1993).

Analyzing the Tape. Both teachers and mentors will also need to learn how to analyze the tapes. To get the most out of their videotape, teachers should use a three-step process. The process begins by viewing the tape several times alone. In doing so, teachers should avoid focusing on their appearance, a common obsession for most teachers. In viewing the tape, teachers can either take a broad perspective or a focused one. If teachers want a broad perspective that will examine their teaching of that class in general, they should make their own observation notes, using a simple form such as the one shown in Box 9.2. As teachers observe changes in their or the students' behavior, they should make a note of the tape counter, their actions, and the students' actions. If teachers want a focused perspective, looking closely at a specific skill, they should then use one of the specially prepared forms described in Chapter 3.

BOX 9.3

Introduction to Viewing Tape of Teaching

Teacher: Louise Mangels

Date: September 14, 1995

Class

This is a heterogeneous group of 7th graders; their reading scores on the CAT given in Grade 6 ranged from 3.5 to 10.0.

Twenty-nine students are enrolled in the class. On this particular day, 5 were absent.

Unit and Lesson Objectives

We had just started a unit on "Taking It Personally," which was designed to help students respond personally to fiction in a meaningful manner. The lesson objective was to learn how to generate and use questions as guides in reading for the personal response.

Insights in Viewing the Tape

In reviewing the tape for my own professional growth, I first focused on their group interactions as they generated questions. I was pleased with the way they operated as a group, in that I had spent the previous week teaching them the group skills they seemed to have forgotten. In viewing the tape from this perspective, I realized that they will need some further work in handling diversions.

I also felt I was successful in using their questions as guides for the personal response. I have found that having students generate questions to guide their reading and responding is more effective than using textbook questions or making up my own.

In looking at the tape with a critical eye, I think I should have taken less time in checking the quiz. I can reduce that next time by having them check each other's papers from an answer sheet I will prepare.

Suggestions for Viewing

1. Look closely at the group chaired by Sam. They are typical of the class and demonstrate how much they had learned about group skills.

2. Focus also on the method I used to collect and systematize the group questions for class use.

When teachers have finished making either type of record, they should write a few notes to themselves about their general reactions to seeing the tape and recording their observations, such as the following:

Felt I took too long getting into the substance of the class. Still paraphrasing student answers too much; I have to learn how to let the discussion flow, without steering it too much.

Next, they should ask a colleague or their mentor to view the tape with them, giving the viewer some general background information—the nature of the class, the place of that lesson in the unit, objectives for the lesson. The teacher should clarify the purpose of the tape viewing, explaining the type of feedback desired. Three kinds of feedback seem especially useful:

- Data-based feedback on the teacher's use of a particular skill. Teachers ask the viewer to use one of the specially prepared forms.
- Questions that will help teachers reflect about important interactions. Teachers ask the viewer to stop the tape any time a significant teacher-student behavior occurs and ask the teacher a question that will help him or her think about the interaction.
- The colleague's opinion as to which parts of the tape would be best to include in any portfolio that the teacher is preparing. In general, teachers should avoid asking the viewer to evaluate their teaching. Most peers are so reluctant to evaluate that they will offer only praise.

Box 9.3 shows a summary that the teacher could prepare for a professional who is to view the tape.

Additional Resources

Books

Frase, L. E., & Conley, S. C. (1994). *Creating learning places for teachers, too.* Thousand Oaks, CA: Corwin.

Grimmett, P. P., & Neufeld, J. (Eds.). (1994). *Teacher development and the struggle for authenticity.* New York: Teachers College Press.

Livingston, C. (Ed.). (1992). *Teachers as leaders: Evolving roles.* Washington, DC: National Education Association.

Smith, S. C., & Scott, J. J. (1990). *The collaborative school.* Eugene: University of Oregon, ERIC Clearinghouse on Educational Management.

Walling, D. R. (Ed.). (1994). *Teachers as leaders: Perspectives on the professional development of teachers.* Bloomington, IN: Phi Delta Kappa.

Multimedia

The following multimedia resources are listed according to the publisher. Association for Supervision and Curriculum Development, 1250 N. Pitt Street, Alexandria, VA 22314.

How to Plan and Implement a Peer Coaching Program (audio)

How to Help Beginning Teachers (video)

Shared Decision Making (video)

Teaching to Learning Styles (video)

Toward a Community of Learning (audio)

National Staff Development Council, Box 240, Oxford, OH 45056.

Instructional Solutions (computer software)

Strategies for Effective Instruction (video)

Supporting New Teachers (audio)

Teaching Episodes (video)

Phi Delta Kappa, Box 789, Bloomington, IN 47402.

Inducting New Teachers Into the Profession (video)

Maintaining Teacher Effectiveness (video)

Motivation and the Teacher (video)

References

Barnett, B. G. (1990). Peer-assisted leadership. *Journal of Educational Administration, 28*(3), 67-76.

Beckham, J. C. (1981). *Legal aspects of evaluation.* Topeka, KS: National Organization on Legal Problems in Education.

Berliner, D. C. (1986). In search of the expert pedagogue. *Educational Researcher, 15*(7), 5-13.

Berryman, S. E. (1991). *Cognitive science: Challenging schools to design effective learning environments.* New York: Institute on Education and the Economy, Columbia University.

Blase, J., & Kirby, P. C. (1992). *Bringing out the best in teachers.* Newbury Park, CA: Corwin.

Bracey, G. W. (1994). The fourth Bracey report on the condition of public education. *Phi Delta Kappan, 76*, 115-127.

Bridges, E. M. (1990). What to do with problem teachers: Managerial responses to poor performance. In S. B. Bacharach (Ed.), *Education reform: Making sense of it all* (pp. 370-378). Boston: Allyn & Bacon.

Bridges, E. M. (1992). *The incompetent teacher: Managerial responses.* Washington, DC: Falmer.

Brooks, J. G., & Brooks, M. G. (1993). *In search of understanding: The case for constructivist classrooms*. Alexandria, VA: Association for Supervision and Curriculum Development.

Burden, P. R. (1982, February). *Developmental supervision: Reducing teacher stress at different career stages*. Paper presented at the annual meeting of the Association of Teacher Educators, Phoenix, AZ.

Byrne, B. M. (1994). Burnout: Testing for the validity, replication, and invariance of causal structure across elementary, intermediate, and secondary teachers. *American Educational Research Journal, 31,* 645-673.

Carson, C. C., Huelskamp, R. M., & Woodall, T. D. (1992). Perspectives on education in America: An annotated briefing. *Journal of Educational Research, 86,* 259-310.

Christensen, J., Burke, P., Fessler, R., & Hagstrom, D. (1983). *Stages of teachers' careers: Implications for professional development*. Washington, DC: ERIC Clearinghouse on Teacher Education.

Collins, A., Brown, J. S., & Newman, S. (1989). Cognitive apprenticeships: Teaching the craft of reading, writing, and mathematics. In L. B. Resnick (Ed.), *Knowing, learning, and instruction: Essays in honor of Robert Glaser* (pp. 453-494). Hillsdale, NJ: Lawrence Erlbaum.

Conley, S. C., & Cooper, B. S. (1991). *The school as a work environment*. Boston: Allyn & Bacon.

Corcoran, T. B. (1990). Schoolwork: Perspectives on workplace reform. In M. W. McLaughlin, J. E. Talbert, & N. Bascia (Eds.), *The contexts of teaching in secondary schools* (pp. 142-166). New York: Teachers College Press.

Cross, K. P. (1981). *Adults as learners*. San Francisco: Jossey-Bass.

Cunningham, W. G., & Gresso, D. W. (1993). *Cultural leadership: The culture of excellence in education*. Boston: Allyn & Bacon.

Devaney, K. (1987). *The lead teacher: Ways to begin*. New York: Carnegie Forum on Education and the Economy.

Doyle, W. (1986). Classroom organization and management. In M. C. Wittrock (Ed.), *Handbook of research on teaching* (3rd ed., pp. 392-432). New York: Macmillan.

Dunn, T. G., Taylor, C. A., Gillig, S. E., & Henning, M. J. (1987, April). *Experience, expertise, and teacher planning*. Paper presented at the annual meeting of the American Educational Research Association, Washington, DC.

Duttweiler, P. C. (1988). *Organizing for excellence.* Austin, TX: Southwest Educational Development Laboratory.

Eckart, J. A., & Gibson, S. L. (1993). Using camcorders to improve teaching. *Clearing House, 66,* 288-292.

Elam, S. M., Rose, L. C., & Gallup, A. M. (1994). The 26th annual Phi Delta Kappa/Gallup poll of the public's attitudes toward the public school. *Phi Delta Kappan, 76,* 41-56.

Fay, C. (1992). Empowerment through leadership. In C. Livingston (Ed.), *Teachers as leaders: Evolving roles* (pp. 57-90). Washington, DC: National Education Association.

Freiberg, H. J., & Knight, S. L. (1991). Career ladder programs as incentives for teachers. In S. C. Conley & B. S. Cooper (Eds.), *The school as a work environment: Implications for reform* (pp. 203-220). Boston: Allyn & Bacon.

Fullan, M. (1994). Teacher leadership: A failure to conceptualize. In *Teachers as leaders: Perspectives on the professional development of teachers* (pp. 241-254). Bloomington, IN: Phi Delta Kappa.

Galvez-Hjornevik, C. (1986). Mentoring among teachers: A review of the literature. *Journal of Teacher Education, 37*(1), 121-126.

Glatthorn, A. A. (1990). *Supervisory leadership.* New York: HarperCollins.

Glatthorn, A. A. (1993). *Learning twice: An introduction to the methods of teaching.* New York: HarperCollins.

Glatthorn, A. A. (in press). Roles, responsibilities, and relationships. In G. R. Firth & E. F. Pajak (Eds.), *Handbook of research on school supervision.* New York: Scholastic.

Glickman, C. D. (1991). Pretending not to know what we know. *Educational Leadership, 48*(8), 4-10.

Good, T. L., & Brophy, J. E. (1991). *Looking in classrooms* (5th ed.). New York: HarperCollins.

Griffey, D., & Housner, L. P. (1985, April). *Differences between novice and expert teachers' planning decisions, interactions, and student engagement.* Paper presented at the annual meeting of the American Educational Research Association, Chicago, IL.

Hargreaves, A. (1992). Cultures of teaching: A focus for change. In A. Hargreaves & M. G. Fullan (Eds.), *Understanding teacher development* (pp. 216-240). New York: Teachers College Press.

Huberman, M. (1989). The professional life cycle of teachers. *Teachers College Record, 91,* 31-57.

Hunter, M. (1984). Knowing, teaching, and supervising. In P. L. Hosford (Ed.), *Using what we know about teaching* (pp. 69-192). Alexandria, VA: Association for Supervision and Curriculum Development.

Jacullo-Noto, J. (1987, April). *Teachers: Behavioral characteristics of emerging leaders.* Paper presented at the annual meeting of the American Educational Research Association, Washington, DC.

Johnson, S. M. (1990). *Teachers at work: Achieving success in our schools.* New York: Basic Books.

Joyce, B., & Weil, M. (1986). *Models of teaching* (3rd ed.). Englewood Cliffs, NJ: Prentice Hall.

Knowles, M. (1984). *The adult learner: A neglected species* (3rd ed.). Houston, TX: Gulf.

Kowalski, T. J., & Weaver, R. A. (1987, April). *Characteristics of outstanding teachers: An academic and social involvement profile.* Paper presented at the annual meeting of the American Educational Research Association, Washington, DC.

Kuralt, R. C. (1987). The computer as a supervisory tool. *Educational Leadership, 44*(7), 71-72.

Lambert, L. (1984, April). *How adults learn.* Paper presented at the annual meeting of the American Educational Research Association, New Orleans, LA.

Lawrence, C. E., Vachon, M. K., Leake, D. O., & Leake, B. H. (1993). *The marginal teacher: A step-by-step guide to fair procedures for identification and dismissal.* Newbury Park, CA: Corwin.

Lee, G. V. (1987). Instructional leadership in a junior high school: Managing realities and creating opportunities. In W. Greenfield (Ed.), *Instructional leadership: Concepts, issues, and controversies* (pp. 75-99). Boston: Allyn & Bacon.

Leithwood, K. A. (1992). The principal's role in teacher development. In M. Fullan & A. Hargreaves (Eds.), *Teacher development and educational change* (pp. 86-103). Washington, DC: Falmer.

Levine, M. (Ed.). (1992). *Professional practice schools: Linking teacher education and school reform.* New York: Teachers College Press.

Lieberman, A. (1992). Teacher leadership: What are we learning? In C. Livingston (Ed.), *Teachers as leaders: Evolving roles* (pp. 159-166). Washington, DC: National Education Association.

Loucks-Horsley, S., Harding, C. K., Arbuckle, M. A., Murray, L. B., Dubea, C., & Williams, M. K. (1987). *Continuing to learn: A guidebook for teacher development.* Andover, MA: Regional Laboratory for Educational Improvement of the Northeast and Islands.

Louis, K. S. (1992). Restructuring and the problem of teachers' work. In A. Lieberman (Ed.), *The changing contexts of teaching* (pp. 138-156). Chicago: University of Chicago Press.

Maehr, M. L., Smith, J., & Midgley, C. (1990). *Teacher commitment and job satisfaction.* Urbana: National Center for School Leadership, University of Illinois at Urbana-Champaign.

Marzano, R. J. (1992). *A different kind of classroom: Teaching with dimensions of learning.* Alexandria, VA: Association for Supervision and Curriculum Development.

McLaughlin, M. W. (1994). Strategic sites for teachers' professional development. In P. G. Grimmett & J. Neufeld (Eds.), *Teacher development and the struggle for authenticity* (pp. 31-51). New York: Teachers College Press.

McLaughlin, M. W., & Pfeifer, R. S. (1988). *Teacher evaluation: Improvement, accountability, and effective learning.* New York: Teachers College Press.

McLaughlin, M. W., & Yee, S. M. (1988). School as a place to have a career. In A. Lieberman (Ed.), *Building a professional culture in schools* (pp. 23-44). New York: Teachers College Press.

Miller, L. (1992). Teacher leadership in a renewing school. In C. Livingston (Ed.), *Teachers as leaders: Evolving roles* (pp. 115-130). Washington, DC: National Education Association.

Pickard, P. W. (1993). How to work with the library media specialist: A new perspective. *Tips for principals.* Reston, VA: National Association of Secondary School Principals.

Rogers, S. (1987). If I can see myself, I can change. *Educational Leadership, 44*(2), 64-67.

Ropo, E. (1987, April). *Teachers' conceptions of teaching and teaching behavior: Some differences between expert and novice teachers.* Paper presented at the annual meeting of the American Educational Research Association, Washington, DC.

Rosenholtz, S. J. (1989). *Teachers' workplace: The social organization of schools.* New York: Longman.

Schlechty, P., & Vance, V. (1983). Recruitment, selection, and retention. *Elementary School Journal, 83*, 469-487.

Scott, J. J., & Smith, S. C. (1987). *From isolation to collaboration: Improving the work environment of teaching.* Eugene, OR: ERIC Clearinghouse on Educational Management.

Sergiovanni, T. J. (1992). *Moral leadership: Getting to the heart of school improvement.* San Francisco: Jossey-Bass.

Sergiovanni, T. J. (1994). *Building community in schools.* San Francisco: Jossey-Bass.

Smith, W. F., & Andrews, R. L. (1989). *Instructional leadership: How principals make a difference.* Alexandria, VA: Association for Supervision and Curriculum Development.

Spielberger, C. D. (1992). Learner-centered psychological principles: Guidelines for school redesign and reform. *Psychology Teacher Network, 2*(2), 5-12.

Sprinthall, N. A., & Thies-Sprinthall, L. (1983). The teacher as adult learner: A cognitive-developmental view. In G. A. Griffin (Ed.), *Staff development* (82nd yearbook of the National Society for the Study of Education, Part II, pp. 13-35). Chicago: University of Chicago Press.

Stickel, S. A. (1990, February). *A study of role congruence between school counselors and school principals* (ERIC Document Reproduction Service No. ED 321 944). Paper presented at the annual meeting of the Eastern Educational Research Association, Clearwater, FL.

Stiggins, R. J., & Duke, D. (1988). *The case for commitment to teacher growth.* Albany, NY: SUNY.

Stodolsky, S. S. (1984). Teacher evaluation: The limits of looking. *Educational Researcher, 13*(3), 11-18.

University of North Carolina Model Clinical Teaching Network. (1992). *Learning to teach in North Carolina.* Chapel Hill, NC: Author.

Veenman, S. (1984). Perceived problems of beginning teachers. *Review of Educational Research, 54*, 143-178.

Wasley, P. A. (1991). *Teachers who lead: The rhetoric of reform and the realities of practice.* New York: Teachers College Press.

Index

characteristics of, 57-59
competency of, 4, 13, 39, 57-59,
71-74
conferences with, 62-66
development evaluation,
33(table)
intensive development for,
33-34, 36(table), 64-75
intensive evaluation of, 30-33,
62-66
motivation of, 13
observation of, 62-66
portrait of, 55-57
self-directed development of, 35,
36(table)
standard evaluation of, 33(table)
support for, 61-62
See also Marginal teachers;
Passive teachers; Productive
teachers; Quality teaching
Nurses. *See* Special staff

Observation:
as support service, 20-21, 29-30,
31-32
for development, 33-34
of marginal teachers, 81-83, 84-86
of novice teachers, 62-66
See also Conferences; Evaluation

Passive teachers:
and cooperative development,
35-36
beliefs of, 97-98, 100-103
career development of, 13
characteristics of, 13, 93-95
competency of, 13, 39, 93-95
conferences with, 103-105
development evaluation, 32-33
factors influencing, 95-98
intensive development for,
33-34, 36(table)

intensive evaluation of, 30-33
portrait of, 92-93
remedies for, 98-105
self-directed development of, 35,
36(table)
standard evaluation of, 33(table)
work environment of, 96-97,
98-100
See also Marginal teachers;
Novice teachers; Productive
teachers; Quality teaching
Pickard, P., 108
Principals:
and decision making, 18-19
and development programs, 21
and faculty meetings, 19
and individualized supervision,
12-14, 29
and National Association of
Secondary School Principals
(NASSP), 48-49
and novice teachers, 57, 59-61,
62-66, 75(table)
and productive teachers, 45-49,
50, 52, 53-54
and special staff, 106-109, 110-112
authority of, 26(box), 28
leadership of, 16(figure), 22-24,
50
relationships of, 16(figure), 22
routine interactions of, 21-22
See also Conferences; Evaluation;
Observation; Resources
Productive teachers:
and cooperative development,
35-36, 45-46
and principals, 45-49, 50, 52,
53-54
and productivity decline, 52-54
career development of, 13
characteristics of, 13, 44
competency of, 13, 39, 44
development evaluation, 32-33,
46-48

intensive evaluation of, 33(table)
leadership of, 49-52
motivation of, 13, 44
needs of, 45-49
portrait of, 42-44
resources for, 48-49
self-directed development of, 34-35, 36(table)
standard evaluation of, 33(table)
See also Marginal teachers; Novice teachers; Passive teachers; Quality teaching

Quality teaching:
and adult learning, 7-8
and career development, 10-12, 13
and cognitive development, 8
and constructivism, 5-6
and individualized supervision, 12-14, 29
and principals, 12-14, 29
and teacher development, 6-12
defined, 1-2
models of, 4-6
motivation for, 8-10, 13, 44
See also Competency; Learning community; Marginal teachers; Novice teachers; Passive teachers; Productive teachers; Resources; Supervisory services

Resources:
central office, 117-118
for productive teachers, 48-49
for supervisory services, 27(box), 30
instructional materials, 18
National Association of Secondary School Principals (NASSP), 48-49

other principals, 116-117
parents/community, 119-120
school board/superintendent, 114-116
technological support, 120-124
universities, 118-119

Safety, 18
Salary, 17-18
Skill level. *See* Competency
Social workers. *See* Special staff
Special staff:
and cooperative development, 109
and faculty interaction, 109
and principals, 106-109, 110-112
inclusion of, 107-109
monitoring of, 110
problem solving, 110-111
roles of, 106-107, 108(box)
self-directed development of, 109
See also Classified staff
Staff. *See* Classified staff; Marginal teachers; Novice teachers; Passive teachers; Productive teachers; Special staff
Supervisory services:
and principal authority, 26(box), 28
and school values, 26(box), 28
and teacher development, 28, 33-36
and teacher requirements, 27(box), 29-30
constraints on, 26(box), 27-28
development of, 36-41
features of, 26-27(box), 28-29
goals of, 26-27
options for, 30-36
principles of, 25-30
resources for, 27(box), 30

CORWIN
PRESS

The Corwin Press logo—a raven striding across an open book—
represents the happy union of courage and learning. We are a
professional-level publisher of books and journals for K-12 educators, and we are committed to creating and providing resources that
embody these qualities. Corwin's motto is "Success for All Learners."